MW01016865

Hooked on Hockey

Hooked on Hockey

A Spirited Collection of the Game's Great
Stars, Great Moments and More

by Alan Ross

WALNUT GROVE PRESS
Nashville, TN 37211

ISBN 1-887655-87-5

Material for this book was obtained mostly from secondary sources, primarily print media. While every effort was made to ensure the accuracy of these sources, the accuracy cannot be guaranteed. For additions, deletions, corrections or clarifications in future editions of this text, please write WALNUT GROVE PRESS.

Cover Design: Tal Howell
Typesetting: Sue Gerdes

Printed in the United States of America
1 2 3 4 5 6 7 8 9 10 • 99 00 01 02 03 04

ACKNOWLEDGMENTS
The author gratefully acknowledges the friendship, deep support, and opportunity extended by Dr. Criswell Freeman, who makes serious challenge to Wayne Gretzky as the world's biggest Gordie Howe fan. Thanks also to the magnificent staff at Walnut Grove Press and to Karol Cooper for her inspiration and dedicated contributions both on and off the ice during all three periods and an occasional overtime.

Table of Contents

Remembrance

It's hard to forget an experience like going to the old Madison Square Garden in New York for a hockey game in the 1950s. In fact, three times was I lucky enough to see NHL action in the venerable house on 8th Avenue at the gateway to "Hell's Kitchen."

As a boy in Connecticut, it was curious that, other than the New York Yankees, I didn't grow up as a fan of New York teams in any of the professional sports. In hockey, my first love was the Montreal Canadiens, and certainly, it was easy to see why: They were the Yankees of hockey, a towering dynasty from the mid-1950s through the end of the decade, winning an unmatched-to-this-day five consecutive Stanley Cups. My favorite player was Jean Béliveau, "Le Gros Bill," the big all-star center of that magnificent Habs squad. Little did I know then that I was privileged to be peering at history, at future Hall of Famers who are still talked about with reverence in hockey circles: Doug Harvey, the fiery Rocket — Maurice Richard, Boom Boom Geoffrion and Jake "The Snake" Plante, the first goalie to freelance into the corners to clear the puck for his defensemen. Of course, all the world remembers Plante for another more noteworthy contribution — the introduction of the face mask for goalies. And that quite naturally leads me into an editorial comment about the mask.

Don't misunderstand me. If *I* were playing in the nets in the NHL not only would I most certainly wear a mask, I'd demand a full-body suit of steel armor. But there was something almost indescribable about the courageous and heroic way that pre-mask era goalies went through their paces night after night — facing the unknown with the unavoidable lurking terror that, at any split second, their face could be wiped off by a three-inch circular piece of rock-hard rubber rocketing into them at 100 mph. Facial stitches in the hundreds were the rule of the day for the pre-1959 goaltender. Not that today's goalies aren't great athletes and courageous in their own right, but when you define courage on a hockey rink, it begins and ends with the maskless goalkeepers. Period. When I selected my all-time team (see chapter 2), I will tell you with a completely unfettered conscience: I went all the way with candidates from the "in your face" days of goaltending. As it turns out, there was an inarguable beauty or two among them. And that leads me back to my boyhood, back again to Madison Square Garden, where on the night of November 23, 1955, I saw the greatest goalie of all time.

I didn't know of Terry Sawchuk's troubles back then, how the stress of playing 70 full games a season, (something unthinkable in today's two-goalie era) year after year, rearranges a man. Sawchuk had brilliantly opened his career with Detroit, but the night I saw him at the Garden was the first of his two years with Boston. Some say that's when his troubles began — initially through disillusionment at being traded, after leading the Red Wings to three Stanley Cups in four years. But in the seasons that followed, 21 in the league in all, his moods began to run dark and, ultimately, death came prematurely. Few can argue his greatness throughout his career. For the record, that Thanksgiving weekend night back in 1955 found the "mortal" Sawchuk at work — he got rocked by the Rangers 4–0.

A. R.

Introduction

It's a man's game.

— *Gordie Howe*

When I began writing this book, I have to admit I had a preconceived notion about hockey and its delinquent stepchild — violence.

I had grown up with the sport in the mid-1950s and accordingly was comfortable with the role that violence played in the game. Perhaps it's more accurate to say that violence then went unquestioned. Watching Leapin' Lou Fontinato of the New York Rangers and others of his ilk reshape the nose cartilage and facial structure of opposing players was standard bill of fare. An unthinking acceptance of it all pervaded the spectating public.

But like so many on the periphery of hockey, I began to ponder its presence in our modern times. Peoples' views on violence in sports were changing. A friend of mine, a former editor for a national sports publication, recently told me, "Hockey will never be considered a serious sport till they ban fighting. The refs don't even try to break it up. It's WWF. It's a joke." At the time, I agreed. Why promote a carnival atmosphere to the game when it already had everything it needed? Grace, skill, speed...Gretzky had revived the sport as art, why drag in the goons? The game's good enough without it.

But all that was before I began researching the early origins of ice hockey. To my surprise, the one constant throughout the history of the sport, né through the centuries leading up to the game being played on ice, has been fighting — that instinctive physical reaction to anything even remotely perceived as antagonistic. And count on it — hockey has always been rife with misperceptions. There also have been plenty of intentional, willful acts of violence. Marauding Eddie Shore of the Boston Bruins, back in the mid-1920s through the '30s, was the most hated man in hockey for his unrelenting attacks on the ice. Even the great Gordie Howe, someone once said, was called Mr. Hockey to his face and Mr. Elbows behind his back. It's *in* the nature of the game, an inseparable burr in the side of hockey's stylish, elegant thoroughbred.

It's the "fights sell tickets" mentality that needs to be burned at the stake. In the end, it isn't the fights that people remember anyway. It's the flash of a Maurice "Rocket" Richard, the sovereign grace of a Jean Béliveau or Gordie Howe, the artful athleticism of a Wayne Gretzky or Mario Lemieux, the heart-of-a-lion courage of a Terry Sawchuk, Glenn Hall or Jacques Plante, the rink-length dash of a Bobby Orr. That's *really* what people take home from the game.

And the violence? The smart ones like Gretzky just take a seat and shake their heads.

Chapter 1

ORIGINS:
HOCKEY'S BEGINNINGS

Hoquet

Though the true origins of ice hockey are lost in obscurity and must be, unfortunately, relegated to the great Unknown, the implement that we call the hockey stick seems at least to have a point of birth.

The old French had a word, *hoquet*, which means the crook in a shepherd's stick or staff, and the English were known to have banned a sport played with "hockie sticks" in the early 16th century. But the English banned everything back then, "golfe and futeball" most prominently among them. The stodgy British, Parliament especially, apparently saw almost everything recreational as a sinful diversion from duty and task. Thankfully, they have lightened up since then.

Early Skates, Early Stick and Ball Games

Just when the game of hockey left terra firma and eased onto frozen water is another matter of conjecture, with little data to reveal its embryonic mystery.

People have been skating for over 25 centuries — a staggering contemplation, dating back to Scandinavia in the year 5 B.C. Primitive skates were possibly made from the shank or the rib bones of oxen, elk, and reindeer.

Anthropologists unearthed stone tablets in Persia that describe a type of field hockey taking place in Ur of the Chaldea around 2,000 B.C.

The Romans played a game utilizing a leather ball and crooked sticks called *cambucca* back in the second century, but again it appears to have been ground based.

The stakes were extraordinarily high for Irish players of *hurley*, which pre-dates the playing of cambucca: the losers were sacrificed!

Bandy and Hut Kolven

The English game of *bandy*, played with sticks and a ball, more than likely got its name as a derivative of "banned", which was the fate of the sport during the reign of Edward III. Again, there is no hard evidence that this game was played on ice.

However, paintings in Holland in the 17th century depict a game called *hut kolven* being played that unmistakably has the appearance of ice hockey.

The 19th Century's Greatest Team

England, in the village of Bury Fen in Cambridgeshire, claims the honor of holding the longest-known tie to organized ice hockey, dating back to 1813 when they played bandy on ice. The men from Bury Fen played a team from Willingham in 1827. The match was followed by a big feast.

Bury Fen also was holder of a sizeable feat — they were undefeated throughout the 19th century!

In addition to winning home and away matches against at least nine other towns between 1827 and 1860, they won a pair of exhibitions at the Crystal Palace in 1860 and all of their exhibitions on a tour of The Netherlands in 1890-91. By the time of Bury Fen's Dutch tour, though, ice hockey was already solidly entrenched in Canada.

Oh, Canada and the First Game

French explorers came across Iroquois Indians in the St. Lawrence Valley, in 1740, who were playing a game with sticks and a ball that may have resembled field hockey. The English then imported *bandy* and *shinny* sometime around 1830.

The first unassailable evidence of ice hockey's confirmed presence was the awarding of the site of the Hall of Fame of the Canadian Amateur Hockey Association to Kingston, when that city presented empirical proof of having played hockey as early as 1855.

There are several recorded instances during the 1860s and early 1870s, from Kingston Harbour to Ottawa to Halifax, of organized games involving sticks, skates, pucks and goal posts. But it wasn't until March 3, 1875, when two teams of McGill University students, consisting of nine players to a side, faced off against each other at Montreal's Victoria Skating Rink, that the first recorded instance of a game actually referred to as "ice hockey" took place.

Hockey's Early Visionaries

McGill University's W.F. Robertson and R.F. Smith drew up ice hockey's first set of rules in 1879. They borrowed terminology from lacrosse, including the phrase "checking," as well as rudiments of soccer, field hockey, and polo.

Some of the McGill duo's initial rules included: a face-off whenever the puck went behind the goal, nine players to a side, a two-hour time limit, and no body-checking.

Ice hockey, whether it originated (at McGill) or elsewhere, developed out of a process of evolution rather than somebody having invented it.

Frank Menke,
Encyclopedia of Sports

Hockey's Explosion

Regardless of the way in which ice hockey was originally conceived, the explosion of the sport took place in the 1880s in Canada.

In 1885, a four-team league was born in Kingston. Similar enterprises in the cities of Ontario and Quebec soon followed suit, along with league start-ups in the central prairie provinces and Canada's western coast during the 1890s. In Montreal alone there were over 100 hockey clubs by 1895.

Lord Stanley and His Cup

The first link to the hockey that we know and experience today grandly entered the game in 1893 — the Stanley Cup.

Back then, Lord Stanley of Preston, then Governor-General of the Dominion, was persuaded to sponsor a prize that would be looked upon as the symbol of supremacy in hockey; one that could be vied for each year through a competition of challenge rounds. Of course, through the end of the 19th century, all the Stanley Cup winners were teams comprised of amateurs. But that wouldn't last for long.

The First Stanley Cup

Irony of ironies, Lord Stanley never got to see a single Stanley Cup game, having returned to England at the expiration of his term of office in Canada — approximately 10 months before the first actual Stanley Cup match (March 22, 1894: Montreal Amateur Athletic Association vs. Ottawa Capitals). In fact, the first name on the trophy, that of the Montreal A.A.A., was engraved on the direct order of Lord Stanley for Montreal's victory in the Amateur Hockey Association championship the *previous* season, in 1893.

Hockey at the End of the 19th Century

With the Stanley Cup already in place and the game's popularity on a skyrocketing rise, ice hockey entered the 20th century with a look that was still quite different from today's game:

- There were seven players to a side.
- The duration of the game was one hour, but it was broken into two half-periods.
- No substitution was allowed.
- Goalkeepers were required to stay on their feet.
- Offensive skaters had to be behind the puck at all times.
- The size of the goal (4'x 6'), the puck (one-inch solid rubber, three-inch diameter), and hockey sticks (no wider than three inches on the blade) were the same then as they are today.

I can hear the roar of the runners yet, and see the white powder fly as the leader doubled and the whole pack ground their skate blades to the ice and reversed in pursuit. I can still feel the sting of the cold December evening on my hot cheeks as I went for my coat when the game was over...The boys are at it yet, though they all have "store sticks" now, and call the game hockey.

Walter Pritchard Eaton
Outing Magazine, *December 1913*

In past generations, the American athlete of the strenuous type hibernated during the snowy months. After the passing of football, he rested, storing up energy for the opening of baseball season. (However) the youth of today...has crossed the Canadian border and adopted the swift and picturesque hockey as just the sport to fill the season between the two ball games.

Harper's Weekly,
February 1912

Canadians may be said to be born and raised with skates on their feet and hockey sticks in their hands. With constant playing, they learn the things instinctively that all hockey players in this country try so hard to acquire.

Edward Bigelow,
Harvard hockey coach in the late 1920s

Hockey in the USA

The first introduction to hockey in America came in 1893, when Yale and Johns Hopkins universities both instituted the sport, though each brought it in separately. Malcolm Chace and Arthur Foote, the two Yale students responsible for importing the game to New Haven, Connecticut, may also have been instrumental in organizing the first hockey league in the States — the Amateur Hockey League, founded in 1896, in New York City.

The First Pros

Though professionalism first began appearing in Canada's central provinces in the early 1890s, with teams barnstorming on a profit-sharing basis, the first actual professional league — the International Professional Hockey League — wasn't formed until 1904. American franchises were located in Pittsburgh, Portage Lakes, Michigan, and Calumet, Michigan. Sault Ste. Marie fielded teams on both sides of the border, with the Canadian side generally acknowledged as the first-known professional team in Canada.

Six-Man Hockey Arrives

How ice hockey became a six-man game came about quite by accident.

In February 1904, in a pair of games between two of the pioneering professionals — Pittsburgh and the Sault Ste. Marie Canadian team — injuries forced both squads to play with six men each. The result was a faster, more-intense game that fans and owners (for financial reasons) both preferred to seven-man hockey. However, it would take until 1923 for the six-man game to become the norm for hockey everywhere.

The Attacking Goalkeeper

In 1905, Fred Brophy, a goalie for Montreal Westmount, in a game against the Quebec Bulldogs, went the length of the ice with the puck and scored against Paddy Moran, one of early organized hockey's greatest netminders. Brophy duplicated his feat against the Winnipeg Victorias the following season. Perhaps Brophy was a natural forward after all: In 1905, his goals-against average, in six games in the Westmount nets, was a lofty 8.2 per game.

Toronto Maple Leafs — Hockey's Oldest Team By Name

In 1907, the Ontario Professional League debuted with four teams — Toronto, Berlin, Brantford, and Guelph. The Toronto franchise, which took the name Maple Leafs, thus became the NHL team (eventually) with the oldest starting point in hockey history — name-wise, at least — the grandfather of all of today's National Hockey League teams, though it appears to be a line of broken succession.

The current Toronto Maple Leafs trace their heritage back to Valentine's Day 1927, when founder Conn Smythe purchased the Toronto St. Pats franchise and renamed them the Maple Leafs.

The Innovative Patrick Brothers

The Patricks, Lester and Frank, were fine Canadian players in the early 1900s, but ultimately the hockey legacy they jointly carved would come more from their pioneering contributions to the game than for their playing abilities.

As founders of the Pacific Coast Hockey Association in western Canada, the Patrick brothers challenged the eastern establishment National Hockey Association on practically all matters concerning hockey. Finally both leagues mutually began working for change in 1916. The Patricks and their PCHA, however, were the last holdouts to espouse the seven-man game, a format they stubbornly clung to until 1923, when they finally joined the rest of the hockey world in adopting the six-man game as we know it today.

Some of the Patricks' better-known contributions:

- Numbers on uniforms.
- Adopted the bluelines, which broke the ice into three zones.
- Forward passing allowed within each zone (1914).
- Instituted individual scoring records, which included assists.
- Organized selection of first league all-star team in 1914.
- Introduced first left-handed shooter on right wing.
- Goalies allowed to leave feet to stop shots (previously goalies were required to keep their feet at all times) — the advent of the so-called "flopping" goalie.
- Were the first in Canada to invest in rinks with artificial ice.
- Instituted first Eastern vs. Western champion for the Stanley Cup, which ultimately spawned a postseason playoff system.

(Hockey) is a game for men; essentially, it is a game for the youth. It needs strong, full-blooded men. Weaklings cannot survive in it, the puny cannot play it, and the timid have no place in it. It is, perhaps, the greatest game that men can play unaided. It possesses all the spice of polo without the necessity for calling upon the animal kingdom.

Arthur Farrell,
Hall of Fame player and early hockey author,
1910

The First U.S. Stanley Cup Winner

The Stanley Cup in its infancy had been an ongoing series of challenges, sometimes one right after the other in the same season, between Canada's various fractious leagues. Over the years, a league here, a league there would turn belly-up. Eventually, hockey in Canada boiled down to serious year-in/year-out challenges between the NHA (representing the east) and Lester Patrick's Pacific Coast Hockey Association (providing the western champion). One of the big surprises of the pre-NHL days was the one-year ascent of the Seattle Metropolitans to the summit of hockey's ranks. In 1917, the Mets, in only their second year in the PCHA, stunned hockey's eastern establishment by wresting the hallowed Cup from the incumbent champion Montreal Canadiens, three games to one — the first-ever Stanley Cup Finals win by a team from the United States.

"Les Canadiens" Roots

The Montreal Canadiens' lineage dates back to pre-NHL days, when the franchise was located in Haileybury and exercised its rights to the name "Les Canadiens" in 1911. Originally, though, a franchise in Montreal, owned by J. Ambrose O'Brien, a co-founder of the National Hockey Association in 1909, had the "Les Canadiens" name. O'Brien then reportedly gave it to Haileybury, also an original NHA club.

Enter the NHL

The site of many of hockey's league formulations and a center for hockey business, Montreal's Windsor Hotel was once again the location for an historic occasion for one of professional hockey's major milestones — the founding of the National Hockey League, on November 26, 1917.

The birthing of the new league opened with four teams: Ottawa, Montreal's "Les Canadiens," the Montreal Wanderers, and Toronto.

With the advent of the NHL, a virtual stake was driven through the pre-existing NHA.

EARLY GREATS
Newsy Lalonde

Considered the best player of hockey's early era after the turn of the century, Newsy Lalonde was a high-scorer who also had a reputation for physical play. In 1910 he led the fledgling NHA in scoring with 38 goals in 11 games, including nine alone in one game. Back then, players moved from team to team as often as the wind changed direction, but Lalonde only engaged in minimal moving. Early in his stellar career, he was the leading scorer of the original Toronto Maple Leafs, in 1907, in the old Ontario Professional League. Lalonde later would spend 12 out of 13 seasons, from 1910 through 1922, with "Les Canadiens" — from when the team was an original charter member of the NHA through the embryonic days of the NHL itself, which began in 1917.

Throughout his career, Lalonde was the Canadiens' catalyst — invariably the team's leading scorer, clubhouse leader, and No. 1 server of penalty minutes.

He led the NHL in scoring in the league's second and fourth years of existence — 1918-19 and 1920-21.

Frank Nighbor

Some have called him the greatest poke-checker and hook-checker ever. A center, Nighbor was a consistent scorer, and, for his era (1913-1930), one of the great "two-way" players — an offensive threat who could contribute equally on the defensive end of the rink.

Nighbor is best remembered for his 13 years with the Ottawa Senators (in both the NHA and NHL), a team he helped to four Stanley Cup titles.

He was also the very first recipient of the Hart Trophy, given annually to the Most Valuable Player in the NHL, in 1924. In addition, Nighbor was a two-time recipient of the Lady Byng Trophy — emblematic for sportsmanship — the award's inaugural and second winner (1925, '26).

Georges Vezina

The first truly great goaltender in professional hockey history, Georges Vezina, after whom the famous annual trophy for the NHL's top netminder is named, was a legendary figure of endurance and zeal.

Though the award in his honor is largely based upon statistics, Vezina's numbers were humble by today's comparisons. In 15 seasons, he only registered 20 shutouts, but never was there a more courageous player to take the ice in the game's long history. His face and even his eyes were often slashed and cut by flying pucks, but Vezina, in his trademark way, never left the net. Upon hearing of that level of dedication, it lessens the shock to learn that, in his entire career, he *never* missed a regular-season or playoff game.

Almost like the ending of some incredible, dramatic movie, Vezina collapsed in goal in 1925 and had to be carried from the ice. Six months later, he died from tuberculosis, ulcers, and other complications.

Eddie Shore

He was a seven-time first-team NHL All-Star, but that's not what people remember about Eddie Shore.

For 14 seasons (1926-40) Shore terrorized the NHL as the brawling, mauling defenseman of the Boston Bruins. After one particular act of ruthless bludgeoning — the famed Ace Bailey incident (see page 116) — he became known as The Most Hated Man in Hockey. But Shore could absorb the punishment too. During his career he is said to have had 978 stitches taken as a result of 80 wounds; in addition, he broke his nose 14 times and suffered a fractured jaw on five occasions.

Howie Morenz

"He skates *too* fast" was the way one observer put it about the searing speed of the Montreal Canadiens' Howie Morenz.

Morenz became a star in just his second year in the NHL and even gained the respect of Eddie Shore. "He's the hardest player in the league to stop," admitted the Boston bruiser.

From the mid-1920s through the mid-'30s, Montreal with Morenz was the most exciting team on ice. The popularity that he brought to the sport enabled hockey to successfully expand to the United States.

Sadly, in early 1937, Morenz died quickly and somewhat mysteriously from complications, both mental and physical, arising from a severe compound leg fracture suffered in a game against Chicago.

Chapter 2

THE BEST EVER: HOCKEY'S ALL-TIME TEAM

Hockey's All-Time Team

This team of unparalleled all-stars would likely paralyze any opposition placed in its way, simply by taking the ice. Surprisingly, there are few surprises. Only three of the positions leave the possibility for argument. The other three members of this all-time team go uncontested: Gordie Howe, Bobby Orr, and Wayne Gretzky. It's difficult to leave immortals like Maurice "Rocket" Richard, Jean Béliveau and future-immortal Mario Lemieux off the first unit, but that's the natural fallout when you square off superstar against superstar, head to head, legend versus legend.

For your reading and debating enjoyment, here's the crème de la crème — hockey's best six ever.

Hockey's Hallowed Six

Goalie:	**Terry Sawchuk**
Defenseman:	**Bobby Orr**
Defenseman:	**Doug Harvey**
Center:	**Wayne Gretzky**
Left Wing:	**Bobby Hull**
Right Wing:	**Gordie Howe**

In plain English, Terry Sawchuk was the greatest goaltender I have ever seen; that includes old timers to the present. He finished his career with a total of 103 regular-season shutouts. One hundred and three; think about that. And a dozen more in the playoffs. How many goaltenders can make that statement?

> *Johnny Wilson,*
> *Detroit Red Wings,*
> *(1949-55; 1957-59)*

Injuries, I've never really had any — just a few face stitches.

> *Terry Sawchuk,*
> *who, during his 21-year NHL career, took over 400 face and head stitches; suffered severed hand tendons; a broken right arm that didn't mend correctly, leaving it shorter than the other by several inches; a fractured instep; two herniated discs; a severe shoulder separation that permanently limited his arm movement; punctured lungs; ruptured appendix; bone chips in his elbow that required three operations; infectious mononucleosis, and depression.*

Terry Sawchuk is the greatest goalie in the history of league hockey.

> *Frank Boucher,*
> *New York Rangers coach (1939-48; 1953-54)*
> *and general manager (1946-55)*

Terry Sawchuk

The brilliant Detroit Red Wings goalie of the early-to-mid 1950s, as well as from 1957 through 1964, enigmatic Terry Sawchuk played out a star-crossed life.

During his first stint with the Red Wings, he led Detroit to Stanley Cup titles three times in four years. His innovative "gorilla"-style crouch in the goal crease allowed him superior visibility and was especially effective at neutralizing opponents' screens.

But in 1955, Detroit surprisingly dealt the young star to Boston. The trade disillusioned Sawchuk, who seriously considered retirement. Two years later however, Detroit, realizing the error of its ways, traded again for the talented netminder.

Until 1962, Sawchuk tended goal without a face mask — by anyone's definition a superior standard for courage — taking over 400 stitches in his face and head. His phenomenal 103 shutouts are still an NHL record. During his 21-year career in which he played for four other teams besides Detroit, Sawchuk either won outright or shared the Vezina Trophy four times. On five occasions he was a member of a Stanley Cup championship team.

But none of that could spare the troubled goaltender from his increasing mental malaise. After his problems drove away his wife and children, Sawchuk's life suddenly and prematurely came to an end in May of 1970 — the result of repercussions from an altercation with Rangers teammate — and roommate — Ron Stewart.

Doug Harvey was the greatest defenseman who ever played hockey — bar none.

Toe Blake,
Montreal Canadiens player (1935-48),
head coach (1955-68)

Doug Harvey

The steadying if unspectacular defensive force who was the bedrock of the amazing Montreal Canadiens dynasty of the 1950s, Doug Harvey's talents were often overshadowed by the greatness of teammates Jean Béliveau, Maurice Richard, Bernie "Boom Boom" Geoffrion, and goalie Jacques Plante.

Not known as a scoring defenseman, Harvey's forte was cool execution and uncanny control. Unlike Eddie Shore, Lou Fontinato and others, he was no brawler. But Harvey's stick-handling skills, particularly on the power play, and accurate passing enabled him to log 432 assists in 1,043 games. On defense, he was a master at forcing opponents to make the first move, the essence of true defensive hockey. His superior skating speed could also help him control the tempo of a game — picking it up or slowing it down to offset the other team's rhythm.

Harvey was a 10-time first-team NHL All-Star and seven-time Norris Trophy winner in his 19 seasons as a player, 14 of them with Montreal. Six times he helped hoist the Stanley Cup in victory with the Canadiens.

Howe could do everything but not at top speed. Hull went at top speed but couldn't do everything. Orr can do everything, and do it at top speed.

Harry Sinden,
Boston Bruins coach (1966-70; 1979-80; 1984-85),
general manager (1972-)

Orr is a stylish, graceful athlete who does everything extremely well, much in the manner of Joe DiMaggio.

Robert Markus,
Chicago Tribune

I've been around for 15 years and thank God I've finally won it (Norris Trophy). I've got a feeling that for the next 20 years it will be known as the Bobby Orr Trophy.

Harry Howell,
New York Rangers defenseman (1952-69)

Bobby Orr

He was, simply, incomparable. Not even The Great Gretzky, it is said, was his equal. Bobby Orr redefined the role of the defenseman in hockey forever, with his end-to-end scoring dashes and tactical creativity.

Instant acceleration and a fluidity in skating that separated him from the pack marked Orr's rink presence. Opponents never knew what to expect when he headed up ice with the puck.

Though he won his first Norris Trophy after only his second season with Boston, it was during his fourth campaign (1969-70) that Orr took his level of play to the ionosphere. That year he won every major trophy in the sport except the Vezina (for goaltenders) and the Calder (for rookies, which he wasn't eligible for). It is considered the greatest single season a player ever put together: Orr won the Hart (league MVP), Art Ross (scoring champ), Norris (top defenseman) and Conn Smythe (playoff MVP) trophies, *plus* the Stanley Cup as a member of the winning Bruins. In overtime of Game 4 of that Cup series, he scored what many consider to be the most famous goal in hockey history to win Boston's first Stanley Cup title in 29 years.

Sadly, Orr's magnificent career came to a relatively early end due to chronic knee problems. In his 12 seasons, he went through six operations on his left knee. At the age of 30, Orr was forced to retire.

 A sk a fifty-goal scorer what the goalie looks like, and he'll say the goalie's just a blur. Ask a five-goal scorer and he'll tell you the brand name of the pad of every goalie in the league. I'm seeing the net, he's seeing the pad.

Wayne Gretzky

 A fire hydrant could get 40 goals playing with Wayne Gretzky.

Glen Sather,
Edmonton Oilers coach (1977-89; 1993-94)

Wayne Gretzky

The Great One is no misnomer. Wayne Gretzky has left a trail of NHL records from here to Toronto (home of the Hockey Hall of Fame) and will go down in history as one of the game's two or three greatest players ever.

In only his 11th season in the league, Gretzky surpassed hockey's No. 1 all-time milestone: Gordie Howe's previously thought-to-be-impassible career points total of 1,850 — all the more remarkable in that it took Howe *26* campaigns to accrue his total.

By the midpoint of his 19th season in the NHL, Gretzky had set or tied *61* regular-season, playoff, and All-Star scoring records combined. He has taken the Hart Trophy for league MVP an unfathomable nine times and claimed the Art Ross Trophy as NHL scoring leader an unprecedented 10 times.

To make a Great situation even Greater, Gretzky is considered a gentleman's gentleman and his activities off ice to benefit others are legendary.

Gretzky, not regarded as an extraordinary skater or shooter, has an uncanny sixth sense that always finds him in the optimal position to make a play. In an age when sheer physical power has come to define the game, Gretzky reintroduced the finesse player — the smooth, lyrical talent that is at once graceful and artistic...and deadly productive.

Hull is a combination of both Richard and Howe. Hull has Howe's explosive speed and his strength and durability. He can skate faster than either one and he shoots harder.

Bill Reay,
Chicago Blackhawks coach (1963-77)

Bobby Hull

The most prolific left wing in NHL history, the "Golden Jet" still ranks among the top ten goal-scorers of all time, well over a quarter of a century since leaving the Chicago Blackhawks for a seven-year run in the WHA.

Hull's outstanding abilities gained him two major distinctions during his halcyon days in the Windy City: He was clocked as the fastest man in hockey carrying the puck, in a mercurial 29.4 mph. Secondly, his slap shot was recorded as the hardest shot in the game — timed at 118.3 mph, a full *35* mph faster than the league average.

Hull became only the third player ever, behind the Canadiens' Maurice Richard and Boom Boom Geoffrion, to record 50 goals in a season, a feat he performed five times. He twice won the Hart Trophy as league MVP and claimed three Art Ross Trophies as the NHL scoring champion. Hull was a 10-time first-team NHL All-Star.

Howe makes the difficult plays look easy, routine. You can't miss the skill of a player like Maurice Richard, it's so dramatic! Gordie — you have to know your hockey or you won't appreciate him.

Tommy Ivan,
Detroit Red Wings coach (1947-54)

Gordie played in an All-Star game when he was 52. I know *I* won't be playing in an All-Star game when I'm 52. I'll be laying on a beach in Tahiti watching Gordie play in it.

Wayne Gretzky

Noted hockey writer Stan Fischler was once asked to pick three All-Star teams: one for the Past, one for the Present, and one for the Future. "Start with Gordie Howe," Fischler said. "Put him on all three."

George Sullivan,
author, Face-Off!

Gordie Howe

I've always felt there was one certain nickname above all others in the colorful sea of sports sobriquets — the one beginning with the respectful prefix "Mr." that indicates the person mentioned is the essence of the sport itself. Take "Mr. Hockey" for example. Only one name in rink lore comfortably fills *that* slot — Gordie Howe. In his spectacular 32-season career (26 NHL, 6 WHA), Howe set virtually every career scoring mark. Of course, Wayne Gretzky has since seized control of all his old hero's records, but Howe's legacy was built on more than just points.

For 25 years the tough, gritty, hugely talented right winger of the Detroit Red Wings (1946-71) ruled hockey as its classiest and hardest-working competitor. Six times he was named league MVP and six times he was top scorer. Howe was also a 12-time first-team NHL All-Star selection and was the star of four Stanley Cup championship teams in the early 1950s, when the Wings had their strongest years.

The greatest moments for Howe personally came in his second pro stint, from 1973 to 1979, in the old World Hockey Association. There he got the chance to play with sons Mark and Marty, forming the front line of the Houston Aeros and, later, the New England Whalers. The trio made its mark, leading Houston to two Avco Cups, the equivalent of the Stanley Cup in the WHA. Howe's presence brought a credibility to the young league that helped it gain recognition and, ultimately, merge in 1979-80 with the NHL.

Second All-Time Team

Goalie: **Glenn Hall** (Det., Chi., St. Louis)

Defenseman: **Ray Bourque** (Boston)

Defenseman: **Eddie Shore** (Boston)

Center: **Mario Lemieux** (Pittsburgh)

Left Wing: **Ted Lindsay** (Det., Chi.)

Right Wing: **Maurice "Rocket" Richard** (Mont.)

Third All-Time Team

Goalie: **Vladislav Tretiak** (USSR)

Defenseman: **Red Kelly** (Det., Tor.)

Defenseman: **Denis Potvin** (NY Islanders)

Center: **Jean Béliveau** (Mont.)

Left Wing: **Mark Messier** (Edm., NYR, Van.)

Right Wing: **Mike Bossy** (NY Islanders)

Chapter 3

THE GOLDEN AGE OF THE ORIGINAL SIX (1942 - 1967)

The Original Six

The name evokes an image of a brood of newly hatched chicks struggling to get up on their feet for the long road ahead.

In fact, the National Hockey League *did* struggle in its inceptive years, barely keeping its gasping head above water. It was a turbulent time of constant change and never-ending rules changes. And contrary to the name "the Original Six," only four clubs were in place for the league's start-up in 1917. At midseason of that inaugural campaign, the Montreal Wanderers, a charter NHL member and cornerstone of pro hockey's pre-NHL era, folded, leaving just a three-team configuration in the league. It got worse.

In 1918-1919, the Toronto franchise went under, and then there were just two teams. As a result of the attrition, the second half of the regular-season schedule was abandoned and, through a bizarre set of circumstances (and for the only time in its long history), there was no Stanley Cup that year. Toronto regained its footing for the following season, coming out as the St. Patricks, and the Quebec Bulldogs were also admitted into the NHL, bringing the league once again to four teams.

To add to the confusion, there were other rival professional leagues in western Canada still in existence as late as 1926.

The NHL began to experience surer footing when it eventually tapped the economically desirable United States market, establishing the Bruins in Boston, for the start of the 1924-25 season. A year later, the plum New York market, with its New York Americans, came on board. In addition, a second team in Montreal (the Maroons) and a third U.S. city (Pittsburgh) debuted for the 1925-26 season. An equally big influx took place the following year, in 1926-1927: three new American entries in New York, Detroit, and Chicago brought the total of NHL teams to 10.

But over the course of the next 15 years, the Big Ten was eventually whittled down to the Original Six. It *was* in the year 1942, when the last hanger-on from the old days, the Brooklyn (né New York) Americans, laid down their sticks for the final time, that hockey is said to have entered its "golden" age. Compared to today's expansion circus, these six clubs are the "original" holdovers from an earlier era.

For the next quarter of a century, the Six sunk deep foundations into the game, four of them located in the U.S., and high-level warfare commenced in a perpetual six-team round-robin for pro hockey supremacy. Three of the greatest teams of all-time dominated during that golden era, and immortals such as Gordie Howe, Terry Sawchuk, Maurice "Rocket" Richard, Jean Béliveau, Jacques Plante, Glenn Hall and so many others began their rich legacies.

The Original Six — the Montreal Canadiens, Toronto Maple Leafs, Boston Bruins, New York Rangers, Detroit Red Wings, and Chicago Blackhawks — enjoyed their exclusive reign for a quarter of a century, until a six-team expansion in 1967-68 brought the total number of NHL teams to 12. From then on, expansion became a regular on-going event in the league's pattern of continued growth.

Detroit Red Wings

An "expansion" team brought into the NHL, along with the New York Rangers and Chicago Blackhawks, in the fall of 1926, Detroit began as the Cougars and played its inaugural season not in Detroit but across the river in Windsor, Ontario. The following season, the team began its long reign in downtown Detroit's Olympia Arena on Grand River Avenue. New owner James Norris renamed the franchise the Detroit Red Wings (it had been the Falcons the previous two years) for the 1932-33 season, a chosen inspiration from a team he had once played for called the Winged Wheelers, whose logo was a winged wheel. Norris thought the logo a perfect match for his team and the Motor City.

In the 1942-43 season, the Red Wings opened the official "Golden Age" of hockey by winning their third Stanley Cup overall. Six years later, the club had a run as one of the NHL's most dominant teams ever. From 1948-1955, Detroit won the league's regular-season title seven straight times (still an NHL record) and notched four Stanley Cup championships alongside them. Though they won two more regular-season titles and made the Stanley Cup Finals five more times in the remaining 12 "golden" years, it would be 42 long years before another Stanley Cup was raised overhead by Detroit hands.

The Detroit Red Wings' All-Time "Golden Age" Team:

Goalie:	**Terry Sawchuk**
Defense:	**Red Kelly**
Defense:	**Marcel Pronovost**
Center:	**Alex Delvecchio**
Left Wing:	**Ted Lindsay**
Right Wing:	**Gordie Howe**

New York Rangers

The Rangers began their NHL tenure in 1926 as New York's "other" team, debuting in the league the year after the Americans had opened up the New York market.

The team rang in hockey's golden era as league regular-season champions in 1942, with the front line of Hall of Famer Bryan Hextall, Phil Watson, and Lynn Patrick dominating league scoring. Only two years earlier, New York had won its third Stanley Cup to close out the decade of the 1930s. But World War II began breaking up the club and a 13-year tailspin began. Only twice in that period did the Rangers make the playoffs, one time losing the Stanley Cup Finals to the Detroit Red Wings in seven games (1950). But two players, Buddy O'Connor and goalie Chuck Rayner, became the club's first recipients of the Hart Trophy as league MVP.

Five Hall of Famers — wingers Andy Bathgate, Dean Prentice; defensemen Bill Gadsby, Harry Howell; and goalie Gump Worsley — lifted Rangers fortunes in the 1950s, and by mid-decade they were back in the playoffs. Ironically, just as the golden era waned in 1967, New York began a run of nine consecutive playoff appearances and emerged as a new powerhouse in the late '60s and early '70s. Still, 54 endless seasons passed before the Rangers' Stanley Cup win in 1994.

The New York Rangers' All-Time "Golden Age" Team:

Goalie:	**Gump Worsley**
Defense:	**Harry Howell**
Defense:	**Bill Gadsby**
Center:	**Camille Henry**
Left Wing:	**Dean Prentice**
Right Wing:	**Andy Bathgate**

Toronto Maple Leafs

Toronto closed out the NHL's pre-golden age era with the most dramatic comeback in Stanley Cup history. Down to Detroit three games to none in the 1942 Finals, the Leafs rallied to take the next four games to claim their second Stanley Cup as the Maple Leafs (fifth for a Toronto franchise).

For the first decade of the golden era, the Maple Leafs were truly golden: winning the Stanley Cup six times in 10 years. Though they only took the league's regular-season championship twice in the 25-year period of the Original Six, Toronto carved a gritty reputation for saving its best hockey for the play-offs. Only 14 Leafs were selected to first-team All-NHL teams during the era, the lack of individual recognition rivaling the famous "No-Name Defense"of the NFL's Miami Dolphins of the 1970s.

The golden era spawned eight Maple Leaf Calder Trophy rookies of the year, two Hart Trophy recipients (Babe Pratt, 1944; Ted Kennedy, 1955), and five Vezina Trophy winners (five different goalies).

The Toronto Maple Leafs' All-Time "Golden Age" Team:

Goalie:	**Turk Broda**
Defense:	**Allan Stanley**
Defense:	**Tim Horton**
Center:	**Ted Kennedy**
Left Wing:	**Frank Mahovlich**
Right Wing:	**Lorne Carr**

Boston Bruins

The Bruins were the very first U.S. franchise admitted into the NHL, beginning play in the fall of 1924. They blew into hockey's Golden Age hot on the tail of Stanley Cup championships in 1939 and '41. Boston's Cup-winning years had featured the remarkable frontline trio known as the Kraut Line: Milt Schmidt, Woody Dumart, and Bobby Bauer. During those years, the team also finished as league regular-season champion four consecutive times.

But as was the case with all clubs then in the league, Boston lost quality players to World War II, with many leaving to enlist in the Royal Canadian Air Force and other branches of military service. Throughout the golden era of the Original Six, the Bruins floundered regularly. They rallied briefly in 1957 and '58 to make back-to-back appearances in the Stanley Cup Finals behind the "Uke (Ukrainian) Line" of Johnny Bucyk, Vic Stasiuk, and Bronco Horvath. But the doldrums set in shortly thereafter, when Boston skidded to the bottom, finishing last or in second-to-last place eight successive years.

Not unlike Rip Van Winkle, the Bruins then awoke from their 25-year nap to find the dynastic Bobby Orr era dawning in Beantown in 1967, a prolific period that yielded two Stanley Cup titles and one of the sterling teams in NHL history. During the golden-age era, Boston woefully produced just seven first-team All-Stars.

The Boston Bruins' All-Time "Golden Age" Team:

Goalie:	**Frankie Brimsek**
Defense:	**Bill Quackenbush**
Defense:	**Ferny Flaman**
Center:	**Milt Schmidt**
Left Wing:	**Johnny Bucyk**
Right Wing:	**Bronco Horvath**

Chicago Blackhawks

After winning two Stanley Cups in five years in the mid- to late-1930s, it took another 23 seasons for Chicago to annex its third and, to date, last Cup. From 1938 to 1961, the span between the Blackhawks' second and third Stanley Cup wins, Chicago recorded, incredibly, just *two* winning seasons. Within that same window of time, 17 of the first 18 years of the Golden Age turned up losing seasons for the Hawks. For unmatched futility, Chicago finished in last place nine out of 11 straight years, from 1946 through 1957. They had their moments, but mostly individual ones: In 1943, Max Bentley, who together with fellow sibling, Doug, formed one of the great brother combinations in league history, tied an NHL record by scoring four goals in the same period. On only four occasions did the Blackhawks make the Stanley Cup Finals during the golden-age era.

It's safe to say there wasn't much to shout about until the early 1960s, when Chicago derailed the Montreal Canadiens' roaring express of five straight Stanley Cup winners by ruthlessly intimidating the Habs with ceaseless checking in the 1961 Cup semifinals. The Blackhawks, behind the play of superstars Bobby Hull, Stan Mikita and goalie Glenn Hall, then eliminated Detroit four games to two for their first Cup in 23 years. The Hawks made it to the Stanley Cup final round twice more before the end of the Golden Age in 1967, but only three times since then have they successfully negotiated the Finals, all without victory.

The Chicago Blackhawks' All-Time "Golden Age" Team:

Goalie:	**Glenn Hall**
Defense:	**Pierre Pilote**
Defense:	**Bill Gadsby**
Center:	**Stan Mikita**
Left Wing:	**Bobby Hull**
Right Wing:	**Bill Mosienko**

Montreal Canadiens

One of the three powerhouse dynasties of hockey's Golden Age, the Canadiens stand head and shoulders over their competition for the title of greatest franchise of all time. Much of their legacy was started in the mid-1950s, when the Habs took five Stanley Cups in a row, from 1956-60. No team has ever matched that string for premier consistency. Jean Béliveau, Maurice "Rocket" Richard, Bernie Geoffrion, Dickie Moore, Doug Harvey, and goalie Jacques Plante are all in the Hockey Hall of Fame from that sterling squad.

In fact, the entire decade of the '50s was lorded over by the Canadiens. Though Detroit won three Stanley Cups in the first five years, Montreal was in the Finals *all 10 years*, winning six of them. In the mid-1940s, they salted away Cup crowns in 1944 and '46, behind the scoring power of the "Punch Line" — Elmer Lach, Toe Blake and Richard. But there was extra-added punch too: the incomparable work in goal of Bill Durnan, an all-but-forgotten netminder who, in just seven seasons as a Canadien, won the Vezina Trophy six times and was a first-team All-Star six times. By comparison, Plante, in also winning the Vezina a half-dozen times, logged 12 years in service with Montreal but was only a first-team All-Star on three occasions.

The Canadiens even left their mark at the *end* of the 25-year golden-age era, garnering back-to-back Stanley Cups in 1965 and '66.

The Montreal Canadiens' All-Time "Golden Age" Team:

Goalie: **Bill Durnan**

Defense: **Doug Harvey**

Defense: **Butch Bouchard**

Center: **Jean Béliveau**

Left Wing: **Dickie Moore**

Right Wing: **Maurice "Rocket" Richard**

There are two weak teams in this league and four strong ones...the strong ones are Toronto, Montreal, Chicago and *Gordie Howe*!

Dave Keon,
center, Toronto Maple Leafs (1960-75),
Hartford Whalers (1979)

Chapter 4

SIX GREAT MOMENTS IN NHL HISTORY

We consider Maurice Richard the greatest right wing in the major league, if not the greatest player. I have explicit instructions to meet any price mentioned for Richard's services.

Hap Day,
Toronto Maple Leafs coach,
to Montreal Canadiens GM Frank Selke, 1949

All the money in Toronto wouldn't buy him.

Selke's reply to Day

50 in 50

It was the hockey equivalent of Babe Ruth's 60 home runs in a season or of Roger Bannister's annihilation of the four-minute mile. In the 1944-45 season, the Montreal Canadiens' magnificent Maurice "Rocket" Richard, one of hockey's all-time greats and arguably its biggest box-office draw in the pre-Gretzky era, accomplished an NHL milestone once thought to be unattainable.

On the night of March 18, 1945, against the Boston Bruins' Harvey Bennett, Richard scored his 50th goal in 50 games. The event was hailed as an epic, and observers said it would never be equalled.

That was back during the days of the 50-game regular season. Eventually, teammate Bernie Geoffrion tied the mark, as did Chicago's Bobby Hull. Later, Hull, Phil Esposito, and others surpassed 50 goals in a season. But no one ever accomplished it in 50 games — until Edmonton's all-world Wayne Gretzky shattered it in 1981-82, scoring 50 goals in 39 games, on his way to the current NHL standard of 92 goals in an 80-game season.

Richard was not alone in his record-breaking effort. Canadiens center Elmer Lach registered a then-record 54 assists in the process of feeding the puck to his productive teammate. In accumulating 80 total points, Lach landed the league's season scoring title. The Rocket, though, wound up penning a special page in hockey's great history.

"Flying Orr" Goal Brings Boston First Cup in 29 Years

It was way back in 1941 when Boston last had held the venerable Stanley Cup. After a surprising sweep of the Chicago Blackhawks in the semifinals, the Bruins faced the St. Louis Blues, Stanley Cup finalists for the third successive year. This was the advent of the Bruins' brief dynasty in the NHL and they cut no quarter with the Blues, sweeping the first three games by nothing less than a three-goal margin. However, the superb defensive play of St. Louis forward Jimmy Roberts was holding Boston's young prodigy, Bobby Orr, in check.

But true greats can't ever be totally shut down. Forty seconds into overtime of Game 4, on May 10, 1970, at Boston Garden, Orr took a Derek Sanderson pass from behind the Blues' net and flicked it by "Mr. Goalie," Glenn Hall, for the game- and Cup-winner. Orr was tripped by St. Louis defenseman Noel Picard just after taking the shot, allowing photographers to catch forever the "Flying Orr" soaring past St. Louis' net in mid-flight with stick raised victoriously. Though it was his only goal of the series, Orr logged four assists and claimed the Conn Smythe Trophy as playoff MVP. It climaxed a banner year for the young superstar, who also took home the Hart, Ross, and Norris Trophies for a near-clean sweep of hockey's hardware.

Messier's Hat Trick Propels Rangers Toward First Stanley Cup in 54 years

It had been an eternity — 54 interminable years — since the Stanley Cup last made an appearance in New York City. But on May 25, 1994, the possibility of its long-awaited return moved measurably closer toward becoming a reality, although not before a cardiac case full of close calls.

Led by goalie Mike Richter and all-star defenseman Brian Leetch, the New York Rangers dispatched the New York Islanders and Washington Capitals in the opening rounds. But in the Eastern Conference finals, against their territorial rivals, the New Jersey Devils, things got grim. Down three games to two, the Rangers skated into the Meadowlands Arena for what might be the end of their season. In the previous day's practice, Mark Messier had roused his New York teammates by outright guaranteeing a Rangers victory on New Jersey ice in Game 6. Mess more than fulfilled his promise. Down 2–0 after the first period and 2–1 after the second, the Rangers' captain exploded for a hat trick in the final frame to deliver a memorable 4–2 New York win. In the critical Game 7, the Rangers scored in double-overtime to advance to the Cup Finals against Vancouver.

It was only appropriate that Mark Messier should score the decisive game- and Cup-winning goal in New York's 3–2 seventh-game win over Vancouver, for the Rangers' first Stanley Cup since 1940.

Considering he was hurt, we definitely didn't expect it from him.

Ron Hextall,
Philadelphia Flyers goalie,
on Mario Lemieux's record-tying scoring frenzy,
April 25, 1989

Lemieux's Five Goals in '89 Playoffs

Forty-eight hours before Game 5 of the 1989 Patrick Division finals, it didn't even look like Mario Lemieux would suit up against the archrival Philadelphia Flyers.

In Game 4, Super Mario collided with Pittsburgh Penguins teammate Randy Cunneyworth, suffering a strained neck. But on April 25th, at the Steel City's Civic Arena, the sum total of Lemieux's incredible talent burst on the ice.

Before seven minutes had elapsed in the game, Lemieux already had a hat trick. In the second period he registered three assists plus a fourth goal. He concluded his record-tying night with an open-net goal in the final period — five goals and three assists for a total of eight points! The Penguins easily routed the Flyers, 10–3. Unfortunately for Mario and his mates, Philadelphia would go on to take that series. Pittsburgh's first taste of champagne from a Stanley Cup was still two years away.

Lemieux's memorable goal-splurging effort tied him with earlier-era greats Newsy Lalonde (Canadiens) and Maurice "Rocket" Richard (Canadiens), and modern-era players Darryl Sittler (Toronto) and Philadelphia's Reggie Leach — all of whom fired five goals in Stanley Cup playoff games.

When you win 4–0, and win in four games, there's just not much to get excited about.

Doug Harvey,
Montreal Canadiens defenseman,
after sweeping the Toronto Maple Leafs
for Montreal's record fifth straight Stanley Cup,
1960

Fab Habs Take Record Fifth Straight Stanley Cup

On the verge of making hockey history, the 1959-60 Montreal Canadiens were a runaway train on a one-way track. The Habs had dominated all four previous Stanley Cups, only once dropping as many as two games in the Finals.

But they were far from finished. In 1960, the fabulous Canadiens equalled the phenomenal sweep of eight straight playoff games set by the 1951-52 Detroit Red Wings. In addition, they came close to matching Terry Sawchuk's mark of four shutouts in eight games, blanking the Chicago Blackhawks 4–0 in Game 3 and 2–0 in Game 4 of the semifinals. Coming into the Finals against Toronto, Montreal's Toe Blake was on a 23–2 play-off roll, after taking over as coach in 1955-56. Vezina Trophy-winning goalie Jacques Plante was sensational, recording his third shutout of the playoffs in Game 4, 4–0, to fittingly close out the spectacular sweep. The final page had been gloriously penned on the Canadiens unparallelled five-year run at the top.

C'est magnifique!

Old Man Patrick's Historic Night in Goal

Lester Patrick was the New York Rangers' manager-coach in 1928, after a long and noteworthy career in pro hockey's pre-NHL days as first a player and then a league owner. During that time he had distinguished himself as one of the game's great innovators (see pages 32-33). But when the Rangers' regular goalie, Lorne Chabot, was injured early in the second period of the second game of the 1928 Stanley Cup Finals, Patrick himself, in a shocking move, donned the "tools of ignorance" to mind the Rangers' net in an attempt to help his team stave off the powerful Montreal Maroons.

Patrick was then 44 years old and had long been away from the ice. To add a dimension of the impossible to an already disturbing situation, he had never played goalie before.

What happened next has become legend and rates as one of the great moments in NHL history.

The old man performed incredibly, turning aside every Montreal shot except one. The game then went into overtime, where New York won it at 7:05 into the extra period. Patrick was mobbed. The Rangers went on, no doubt motivated by their coach's inspiring stand-in performance, to eventually win the series in five games. Considered a major upset at the time, the championship was New York's first-ever Stanley Cup.

Chapter 5

THE SIX ALL-TIME GREATEST STANLEY CUP FINALS

Old Stanley

The Stanley Cup, hockey's most prized award that began in 1893, is seven years older than the Davis Cup, emblematic of international supremacy in tennis. Also by contrast, soccer's World Cup, with its Jules Rimet trophy, wasn't instituted until 1930.

Many Called, Few Chosen

A total of no less than 17 different leagues have challenged for the Stanley Cup, before it became the exclusive domain of the National Hockey League in 1926. Though now recognized as the pinnacle point of professional hockey's summit, it was originated as a challenge cup contested for by amateur teams.

6.

Habs Cook Own Goose in Seven-Game OT Thriller

With newcomers Jacques Plante and Jean Béliveau on board (though Béliveau was not yet a major contributor), the 1953-54 Montreal Canadiens looked capable of repeating as Stanley Cup champions. However the Detroit Red Wings had just won their sixth consecutive regular-season championship and boasted league-scoring champion Gordie Howe, while goalie Terry Sawchuk just barely missed winning his third straight Vezina Trophy, by one goal to Toronto's Harry Lumley. The Wings jumped to a commanding 3–1 series lead, but Montreal fought back to tie it all up and force a seventh game. With the score knotted 1–1 at the end of regulation, the game went into sudden-death overtime.

The strangest of incidents ended the battle, lifting Detroit to its second Cup in three years. The Wings' Tony Leswick dumped a high soft shot deep into the Montreal zone, as the team prepared to change lines. The Canadiens' perennial all-star defenseman, Doug Harvey, attempting to glove the puck, instead tipped it past his own goalie, Gerry McNeil, and the championship series was shockingly and swiftly over at 4:29 into the extra period.

For only the second time in NHL history, a Stanley Cup Final was decided in overtime of the seventh game.

He seemed all arms and legs. He turned the Canadiens into an inspired team. No question Dryden was the star. He made fantastic stops.

Ted Green,
Boston Bruins defenseman,
1971 Stanley Cup quarterfinals

5.

Hot Debut for Dryden, Sweet Sayonara for Béliveau

In what would be his last campaign, longtime all-star center Jean Béliveau went out a winner in 1971, crowning his storied NHL career with a 10th Stanley Cup in 18 legendary seasons with Montreal.

The league at the time, though, was under Boston rule. Having swept the Finals the year before, the Bruins failed to repeat as Stanley Cup champions after a record-setting regular season in 1970-71, dropping to the Canadiens in seven games during the quarterfinals, in what is regarded as one of the greatest upsets in hockey history.

Much of Montreal's startling success came from sensational Ken Dryden, a surprise starter in goal after having played only the last six regular-season games. In the Finals against the Chicago Blackhawks, the Habs fell behind two games to none and later trailed 3–2. They were threatening to unravel after Henri Richard's critical comments on Canadiens coach Al MacNeil but regrouped, forcing a seventh game with a spirited 4–3 win in Game 6. The Canadiens then fell in arrears 2–0 in the finale, before Richard's two goals spurred a come-from-behind win for Montreal's 15th Stanley Cup.

Béliveau went out as only royalty should, and the young phenom, Dryden, in an odd twist, was voted the Conn Smythe Trophy — awarded to the playoffs' MVP — a year *before* he would win the Calder Trophy as NHL Rookie of the Year in 1971-72.

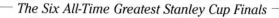

We had the best power play and best penalty-killing, which is a pretty good parlay.

Mike Richter,
New York Rangers'
Stanley Cup-winning goalie,
1994

4.

Rangers End 54-Year Drought

It was the year before the Japanese attacked Pearl Harbor; Joe DiMaggio and Ted Williams were the toast of baseball; and there was no such thing as TV, when the New York Rangers won their third Stanley Cup — in 1940. But the Dark Ages loomed ahead: a sparse 54-year period when no Rangers team would hold the majestic Cup.

All that mercifully ended in the 1993-94 season, when New York finished first in the NHL at the end of the regular season. But a daunting series of playoff foes lay ahead.

Paced by marvelous Mark Messier, a former star with the great Edmonton teams of the mid-1980s, and strongly supported by defensive star Brian Leetch, left wing Adam Graves, and goalie Mike Richter, the Rangers eliminated the New York Islanders and the Washington Capitals in the first two playoff rounds. They had to come from behind in the Eastern Conference championship, defeating the New Jersey Devils in Game 6, thanks to Mark Messier's third-period hat trick. In the deciding Game 7, the outcome went into a nailbiting double overtime, before New York's Stephane Matteau stepped up to notch the game- and series-winning goal.

Against the Vancouver Canucks and their high-scoring star Pavel Bure in the Stanley Cup Finals, the series was excruciatingly stretched to *another* seven games. But the ending couldn't have been more perfect, at least for long-suffering Rangers' fans: New York captain Messier scored the decisive goal in the 3–2 final-game win, and it was party time in the Big Apple.

3.
Toronto Wins "Overtime" Series

Maybe the 1951 Detroit Red Wings expended too much of themselves while achieving an NHL regular-season record of 101 points with only 13 losses all season. Whatever the reason, the Wings were eliminated by a Rocket Richard-led Montreal Canadiens squad that went into the Finals against Toronto in the unfamiliar role of underdogs. In the regular season, Toronto had taken 12 of the 14 meetings between the two.

The '51 Finals are noteworthy for one historical fact: all five games of the series were decided in sudden-death overtime. In the end, Toronto emerged with the Stanley Cup, winning four games to one.

Game 5, the finale, was a classic thriller. The Maple Leafs managed to notch it at 2-all with just 37 seconds remaining, by pulling goalie Al Rollins and adding an extra forward to the attack. In overtime, Toronto defenseman Bill Barilko grabbed a deflected shot at the point just inside the blueline and let fly a blistering slap shot between Montreal's Richard and Butch Bouchard that soared past the shoulder of Canadiens goalie Gerry McNeil for the Cup-winner. Less than four months later, Barilko, the inventor of the hip-check according to former all-star defenseman Brad Park, died in a plane crash at the age of 24.

2.
Sawchuk, Red Wings Take Record Eight Straight

The most dominating performance in Stanley Cup history was executed by the Detroit Red Wings in the 1952 playoffs. They became the first team to ever sweep the Cup semifinals and Finals, dispensing first Toronto then Montreal in devastating fashion.

The indisputable star of both series was Detroit goalie Terry Sawchuk, who recorded shutouts in four of the eight games — a near incomprehensible feat. Against the Leafs, he registered blanks in Games 1 (3–0) and 2 (1–0). That sweep brought to a close the postseason reign of the Maple Leafs. In the previous five seasons, Toronto had claimed the Stanley Cup four times.

In the Finals, the nimble Red Wings netminder encored by logging shutouts in Games 3 and 4 (both 3–0) to climax the most peremptory Stanley Cup ever.

1.

The Greatest Comeback in Stanley Cup History

The 1941-42 Toronto Maple Leafs, down three games to none in the Stanley Cup Finals against Detroit, were facing instant elimination at point-blank range.

They eked out a 4–3 decision on Detroit ice in Game 4. Back home for Game 5, the Leafs suddenly caught fire, holding the Red Wings' productive scoring line of Sid Abel, Syd Howe, and Eddie Wares in check, while they themselves went on a 9–3 tear. Two nights later they blanked the Wings 3–0 to even up the series.

The largest crowd in Maple Leaf Gardens history, over 16,000, witnessed the completion of the greatest comeback in Stanley Cup annals, when Toronto pulled ahead of Detroit in the seventh and deciding game. Behind the clutch play of Sweeney Schriner, who logged two goals in the 3–1 win, and rock-solid goaltender Turk Broda, the Leafs stormed like a stampeding herd to the coveted Cup.

The comeback has since become a source of inspiration to hockey teams of all eras.

Stanley Cup Winners

1997-98	Detroit Red Wings
1996-97	Detroit Red Wings
1995-96	Colorado Avalanche
1994-95	New Jersey Devils
1993-94	New York Rangers
1992-93	Montreal Canadiens
1991-92	Pittsburgh Penguins
1990-91	Pittsburgh Penguins
1989-90	Edmonton Oilers
1988-89	Calgary Flames
1987-88	Edmonton Oilers
1986-87	Edmonton Oilers
1985-86	Montreal Canadiens
1984-85	Edmonton Oilers
1983-84	Edmonton Oilers
1982-83	New York Islanders
1981-82	New York Islanders
1980-81	New York Islanders
1979-80	New York Islanders
1978-79	Montreal Canadiens
1977-78	Montreal Canadiens
1976-77	Montreal Canadiens
1975-76	Montreal Canadiens
1974-75	Philadelphia Flyers
1973-74	Philadelphia Flyers
1972-73	Montreal Canadiens
1971-72	Boston Bruins
1970-71	Montreal Canadiens
1969-70	Boston Bruins
1968-69	Montreal Canadiens
1967-68	Montreal Canadiens
1966-67	Toronto Maple Leafs
1965-66	Montreal Canadiens
1964-65	Montreal Canadiens
1963-64	Toronto Maple Leafs
1962-63	Toronto Maple Leafs

1961-62	Toronto Maple Leafs
1960-61	Chicago Blackhawks
1959-60	Montreal Canadiens
1958-59	Montreal Canadiens
1957-58	Montreal Canadiens
1956-57	Montreal Canadiens
1955-56	Montreal Canadiens
1954-55	Detroit Red Wings
1953-54	Detroit Red Wings
1952-53	Montreal Canadiens
1951-52	Detroit Red Wings
1950-51	Toronto Maple Leafs
1949-50	Detroit Red Wings
1948-49	Toronto Maple Leafs
1947-48	Toronto Maple Leafs
1946-47	Toronto Maple Leafs
1945-46	Montreal Canadiens
1944-45	Toronto Maple Leafs
1943-44	Montreal Canadiens
1942-43	Detroit Red Wings
1941-42	Toronto Maple Leafs
1940-41	Boston Bruins
1939-40	New York Rangers
1938-39	Boston Bruins
1937-38	Chicago Black Hawks
1936-37	Detroit Red Wings
1935-36	Detroit Red Wings
1934-35	Montreal Maroons
1933-34	Chicago Blackhawks
1932-33	New York Rangers
1931-32	Toronto Maple Leafs
1930-31	Montreal Canadiens
1929-30	Montreal Canadiens
1928-29	Boston Bruins
1927-28	New York Rangers
1926-27	Ottawa Senators
1925-26	Montreal Maroons
1924-25	Victoria Cougars

1923-24	Montreal Canadiens
1922-23	Ottawa Senators
1921-22	Toronto St. Pats
1920-21	Ottawa Senators
1919-20	Ottawa Senators
1918-19	No decision
1917-18	Toronto Arenas
1916-17	Seattle Metropolitans
1915-16	Montreal Canadiens
1914-15	Vancouver Millionaires
1913-14	Toronto Blueshirts
1912-13	Quebec Bulldogs
1911-12	Quebec Bulldogs
1910-11	Ottawa Senators
1909-10	Montreal Wanderers
1908-09	Ottawa Senators
1907-08	Montreal Wanderers
1906-07 Mar	Montreal Wanderers
1906-07 Jan	Kenora Thistles
1905-06 Mar	Montreal Wanderers
1905-06 Feb	Ottawa Senators
1904-05	Ottawa Senators
1903-04	Ottawa Senators
1902-03 Mar	Ottawa Senators
1902-03 Feb	Montreal AAA
1901-02 Mar	Montreal AAA
1901-02 Jan	Winnipeg Victorias
1900-01	Winnipeg Victorias
1899-1900	Montreal Shamrocks
1898-99	Montreal Shamrocks
1897-98	Montreal Victorias
1896-97	Montreal Victorias
1895-96 Feb	Winnipeg Victorias
1895-96 Dec	Montreal Victorias
1894-95	Montreal Victorias
1893-94	Montreal AAA

I wish everyone who played hockey could know the feeling of winning the Stanley Cup. You win it once and you get greedy. You want to keep on winning it.

Bryan Trottier,
New York Islanders, 1981

Chapter 6

GREAT HOUSES OF THE ORIGINAL SIX

People talk about the ghosts of Boston Garden. There was so much history in that building, and old-time hockey used to exist there. Players always got up to play in there.

Pat Burns, coach
Montreal Canadiens (1988-92),
Toronto Maple Leafs (1992-96),
Boston Bruins (1997-)

You don't see arenas like that anymore. They've gone the way of the past.

Bobby Hall,
longtime electrician,
Boston Garden

Boston Garden

On November 28, 1928, in front of 16,500, the Boston Bruins hosted the Montreal Canadiens in the inaugural game at Boston Garden, succumbing to the Habs, 1–0. For the next 68 years, the venue would become the focal point of the city's mania over its hockey team.

Quirky irregularities defined the arena's skating area. The surface was nine feet shorter and two feet narrower than standard NHL rinks, but the under-sized conditions seemed suited to Boston's close-checking hard-hitting style of play, first instituted in the 1930s under the violent Eddie Shore and later executed in the late 1960s/early '70s by ice patrollers like Ted Green and Derek Sanderson. The surface size also was tailor-made for the legendary Bobby Orr's rink-length dashes, enabling him to recover defensively after a full-ice rush with the puck.

Old and musty Boston Garden was either unbearably hot (in summer) or downright chilly (in winter). It was also home to the Boston Celtics and came to be distinctly known throughout the world of sports for its unique parquet wooden floor. But its small size, difficult sight lines, high rafters, darkness, and aforementioned chilliness/stuffiness ultimately sounded the gong for the Garden. In 1995, with only the shadows of Shore, Orr, Esposito, Green, the Kraut Line, Tiny Thompson, Frankie Brimsek, Gerry Cheevers, et al. remaining, Boston Garden slipped into memory as the new FleetCenter took center stage for Boston's winter sports.

I remember the old Barton organ they had (at Chicago Stadium) and Al Melgard with his wonderful rendition of "Stormy Weather." He'd hit those low bass keys and make this incredible sound like thunder. It was fascinating!

Don Wojcik,
Chicago sports historian

Chicago Stadium

Not unlike its former brother, Boston Garden, Chicago Stadium bit the dust at the conclusion of the 1994 season, after serving as the hallowed venue of the Chicago Blackhawks for 66 years. The moments of extended glory were few, though three Stanley Cups were claimed there — in 1934, 1938, and 1961. Unquestionably, the Bobby Hull-Stan Mikita era was its finest offering. Another similarity with Boston Garden was the rink's undersized surface — a full 15 feet shorter than the other NHL rinks.

Once surrounded by beautiful brownstones in a comfortable neighborhood, Chicago Stadium, like so many inner-city venues, became a challenge for fans rather than an invitation. Though it seated close to 17,000, it created a cozy environment and even in the steeply elevated second and third balconies, fans felt close to the action. Longtime Blackhawks fan Rich Jegen remembers the incredible sound of the Stadium:

"I'll never forget it. The noise level was just tremendous. Even standing there during the singing of the national anthem — you know how they start cheering toward the end of the song? Well, the swell of that cheer got so loud, it would just roll over you. I can still see Denis Savard down on the ice, waiting attentively through the anthem. I suppose it's more politically correct to wait till the end of it before starting to skate, but man, he'd hear that roar begin and you could tell, a surge of emotion just took over. He would start skating in circles at center ice, like a wind-up toy that was finally let loose."

If an atom bomb landed, I'd want to be in Olympia.

Lincoln Cavalieri,
former general manager,
Olympia Arena, Detroit,
1979

Olympia Arena

"The Old Red Barn" on Grand River Avenue ain't no more. And to hear its former general manager tell it, it's a cryin' shame.

"This is a tremendous building," said Lincoln Cavalieri, associated with Detroit's Olympia Arena for 20 years. "You don't get the charm and the character in a new building that you have here. And the sight lines are the best in the league. We're going to cry our eyes out."

Home of the Red Wings for 53 years, the city boasted that "the arena will stage great spectacles" when it opened in 1927. It delivered its promise.

But it was boxing, not hockey that first brought renown to Olympia. In 1934, a young amateur named Joe Louis made his Golden Gloves debut in the facility and nearly lost. Two historic bouts in 1943 between Sugar Ray Robinson and Jake LaMotta put the increasingly popular venue on the national map.

The heyday of the Red Wings, in the late 1940s to mid-'50s, yielded four of the seven Stanley Cups the team achieved while inhabitants of Olympia. Stars like center Sid Abel and, later, Ted Lindsay, Gordie Howe, and Terry Sawchuk, packed the place.

The structure, built in tiers, was constructed of poured concrete, "not cinder block," reminds Cavalieri. Architectural students once visiting the hallowed hall, after observing the ceiling's fortified trusses, were heard to exclaim, "Wow, we've only seen stuff like that in textbooks!"

When you step on the ice you experience the wonder of a little kid. You're skating around where guys you've admired all your life have skated, our hockey heroes. You see all the Stanley Cup banners in the rafters…it's really special.

Marty McSorley, defenseman,
Pittsburgh Penguins (1983-85),
Edmonton Oilers (1985-88),
Los Angeles Kings (1988-95),
New York Rangers (1995-96),
San Jose Sharks (1996-)

You get a lump in your throat. The *bleu, blanc, et rouge* is everywhere.

Hal Laycoe, defenseman,
New York Rangers (1945-47),
Montreal Canadiens (1947-50),
Boston Bruins (1950-56)

The Forum

It was the Yankee Stadium of hockey. A place where much more than a game on ice took place. It was a shrine, a temple, a hockey house like no other.

The Forum in Montreal *was* hockey. For 72 years it served as the breeding grounds of the game's greatest team, the Canadiens. It spread 22 of Montreal's 24 Stanley Cups over a 63-year period, from 1930-1993. There was a venerable quality to The Forum, a cathedral-like reverence that had players speaking of it in hushed tones.

"You're in awe when you first go in there," said Cesare Maniago, an NHL goalie for 15 seasons. "To see the slogan and all, you just sit down and take it all in without saying too much."

The "slogan" is The Forum's Holy Grail, a sign hanging in the home locker room that bears a line from the poem "Flanders Field": *To you with failing hands we throw the torch, be yours to hold it high.* In importance to French-Canadians, it could rival "Au Canada" if it were an anthem.

The Forum first opened its doors on November 29, 1924, with a rousing 7–1 Montreal victory over Toronto. On March 24, 1936, it hosted the longest game in NHL history: 116 minutes and 30 seconds into overtime the Detroit Red Wings defeated the Montreal Maroons, The Forum's original NHL tenant, 1–0 in the Stanley Cup semifinals.

An august chapter in hockey history was closed on March 11, 1996. Oh, the wraiths still skate at 2313 Ste. Catherine St.— Morenz, Richard, Béliveau, Lafleur— but only as a haunting memory now.

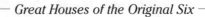

"The Old Lady of Carlton Street" has the venerable feel of a church.

John Davidson,
noted hockey analyst and author,
on Maple Leaf Gardens

Maple Leaf Gardens

The Gardens is far and away the best old house in the National Hockey League. Okay, so it's the *only* one. Gone are the venerable smoky centers of lore in Montreal, New York, Boston, Detroit, and Chicago. Maple Leaf Gardens is the sport's one surviving Rosetta stone. For that alone, it merits sacred status in the league's present era.

The arena was built in the midst of the Depression, in 1931, under the guiding impetus of legendary Leafs founder and coach Conn Smythe. Incredibly, it was completed in only five and a half months.

On opening night, November 12, 1931, the Blackhawks downed Toronto 2–1 before 13,233 awed customers. Floodlights were installed in 1935 and boards replaced the chain-link fence that protected patrons at rinkside in 1947.

Federalist architecture graces the building's exterior on Carlton Street. The roof was completely resurfaced in 1991 with white weatherproofing which is emblazoned with huge blue Maple Leaf logos.

Inside, the original organ loft once featured a mighty Wurlitzer organ and pipe ensemble, and framed pictures of past Leafs greats still adorn the corridor walls. Only two Toronto players' jerseys have ever been officially retired: Bill Barilko's number 5 and Ace Bailey's number 6. Both stars were involved in tragic circumstances that prematurely ended their careers. Their jerseys hang from the rafters, along with the "honoured" numbers of six former Leafs.

Madison Square Garden is, very simply, the most famous and glamorous arena in creation.

Red Smith,
Pulitzer Prize-winning sports journalist

Madison Square Garden

Thanks to a reformed prohibitioner and an ole cowhand, the city of New York held claim to one of the sports world's all-time landmarks.

Though not the original Madison Square Garden (opened by William Vanderbilt on May 31, 1879, on 26th and Madison Avenue), "The World's Greatest Sports Arena," on 8th Avenue between 48th and 49th Streets, on New York's West Side, was built by an ex-wrangler and former Texas marshall named Tex Rickard. William V. Dwyer, a onetime bootlegger who became owner of the New York Americans, the city's first entry into the NHL, convinced Rickard that hockey would sell in his new arena.

Rickard's Madison Square Garden officially opened on December 15, 1925. A black-tie, diamonds-and-furs crowd of 16,000 saw the NHL premier in New York that night, with the Canadiens and Howie Morenz skating to a 3–1 win. Rickard used to send a fleet of ambulances through the streets of Manhattan to stir up interest in this violent new sport (to New Yorkers) called hockey, leaving the fleet curbside in front of the Garden during the Americans' games. Being the natural promoter that he was, and with Dwyer failing to get a non-compete agreement from him, Rickard formed the New York Rangers the following year. That action slowly began to force Dwyer's Americans out of the Garden and eventually to Brooklyn.

Inside the Garden, a miracle of technology was in place: an ice-making system with 12 miles of steel piping imbedded in the facility's terrazzo floor that formed a perfect one-inch-thick sheet of ice. But what made it revolutionary was that it could be broken down in three hours or less for a basketball game, boxing match, track and field games, dog show, or other event.

An endless list of great athletic milestones took place at the old Garden, among them some of hockey's most memorable moments. In 1952, Chicago's Bill Mosienko scored his still-existing NHL-record three goals in 21 seconds against the Rangers in a 7–6 Blackhawks win. It is also where, on the night of November 1, 1959, Canadiens goalie Jacques Plante introduced his historic face mask, forever changing the way goalies equip themselves.

The old Garden gave way to the new one that sits atop Penn Station in downtown New York, on February 11, 1968.

If you're ever on the doorstep of Hell's Kitchen, on the site of the *true* Madison Square Garden, the house that was the Rangers' first home from 1925-1968, squint your eyes. You just might pick out the ghostly forms of Gump Worsley, Chuck Rayner, Harry Howell, the Patricks, Andy Bathgate, Andy Hebenton, Bill Gadsby and Leapin' Lou Fontinato still lurking in the night, like knights in an ethereal Rink of Dreams, calling for the puck just one last time.

Chapter 7

HOCKEY AND VIOLENCE

We have a very violent, emotional game and things are going to happen.

Brian O'Neill
executive vice president,
National Hockey League, 1988

Fighting is part of hockey.

Gerry Cheevers,
Boston Bruins goalie (1965-72; 1975-80),
coach (1980-85)

You know, you're really not a hockey player until you've lost a few teeth.

Anonymous veteran NHL player

Hockey and Violence

There has been an inextricable connection with violence and hockey from the sport's inceptive days. "Mob psychology" ruled early explorations of the game centuries ago.

In the old days, before rules were instituted about stick-raising, there must have been some serious bludgeoning, in what was surely nothing more than organized free-for-alls.

The innate connection with violence seemed natural at the onset — an extra-hard fore check here, an inadvertent slash in the face there, followed by an instinctive retaliatory reaction.

Aggression and macho attitudes are inherent in man's nature. In a game like hockey, the presence of violence can appear almost normal. Add to that the element of skating speed, hard surfaces that surround the playing area, an often-frenzied mob seated immediately beyond the rink, and the equation for violence jumps off the paper...and into your lap!

"The Worst Exhibition of Butchery"

As concern grew for violence that was getting increasingly out of hand, the Montreal Wanderers and Ottawa, in a 1907 game, put on an exhibition of incredible brutality. One Ottawa player "used his stick like a bat" across the temple of the Wanderers' Hod Stuart, who is credited with being hockey's first attacking defenseman, à la Bobby Orr. In this case, though, Stuart was more the attack*ee*. Lastly, one more Ottawa player was described as using his hockey stick "like a war club" in breaking the nose of yet another Montreal player. The next day the *Montreal Star* reported the contest as "the worst exhibition of butchery among hockey brutalities." For the record, two of the offending Ottawa players were fined $20 each and placed on probation for a year.

Well, Since There Was More Than One of You, I Guess a Little Murder Is Okay

A worse disaster followed in the embroiled 1907 season. The Federal Amateur Hockey League's leading scorer, Owen McCourt, got involved in a brawl in a league game on March 6. He left the ice with a bleeding head wound that allegedly came from the stick of Charles Masson. McCourt lost consciousness and died the following day, and Masson was brought to trial on murder charges, later reduced to manslaughter. But the defendant gained an acquittal from a Judge Mager, who dismissed the charges when it was learned through witness testimony that other sticks, earlier than Masson's, had reached McCourt's head.

Hockey's Most Famous Case of Violence: The Ace Bailey Incident

On the night of December 12, 1933, at Boston Garden, an extraordinarily violent affair made its way into the dubious pages of hockey history.

The Boston Bruins' infamous Eddie Shore, the belligerent bully of the era, was the antagonist. His victim, and an innocent one at that, was Toronto Maple Leafs left winger Ace Bailey.

Halfway into the second period, Shore was slammed into the boards by Toronto's Red Horner (some accounts say it was King Clancy), but Shore at the time of the check didn't know who his aggressor was. Seeing red, the short-fused Shore attacked the first player he saw in blue and white. It was a case of being in the wrong place at the wrong time for Bailey. Leveled from behind, the Maple Leafs winger fell head over heels, landing with a horrifying thud on his head. His body immediately went limp. Bailey had suffered a serious hematoma and blood began clotting quickly. Two brain surgeries were required to relieve the pressure of building fluid, and the player hovered near death for days. But Bailey, though he was finished with hockey, eventually recovered and even forgave Shore publicly.

As a result of the incident, Shore became the most booed player of all time in hockey.

Red Sullivan's Last Rites

Once forewarned, twice...well, better look out if you make your living in the NHL.

In the 1950s, the Canadiens' nonpareil defenseman, Doug Harvey (see chapter two: the all-time team), who was not especially known for physical play, had warned the New York Rangers' Red Sullivan to stop the dangerous practice of kicking the skates out from underneath the Montreal star whenever they went into the corners after a loose puck.

When Sullivan failed to heed the warning, Harvey waited for the opportune moment to "speak" back. It came when the Rangers veteran center led a charge down the ice. Just after crossing the red line into Montreal's end of the ice, Sullivan passed off to a teammate. While attention was focused elsewhere, Sullivan suddenly went down, doubled up on the ice — the victim of spearing from Harvey's blade end of his stick.

The attack nearly severed Sullivan's spleen. He was rushed to the hospital and was even given last rites, a "closing" ceremony usually administered to Catholics on their death bed.

Sullivan, however, fortunately survived and went on to continue his five-year career (1956-61) with New York.

Howe Out-Points Hockey's "Heavy-weight Champion"

The NHL's No. 1 badman back in the 1950s was a slugging defenseman for the New York Rangers named Lou Fontinato.

One night, Fontinato skated over 70 feet to the rescue of teammate Eddie Shack, who had gotten entangled in an altercation with the great Gordie Howe. Fontinato slammed into Howe from behind, taking the Red Wings ace by surprise. The Ranger bully then unleashed a series of blows that would have finished off most men. But Howe, though staggered, weathered the worst of the attack and somehow managed to recover. Then it was his turn. The Detroit legend, a tough man and renowned pugilist in his own right, retaliated with a bevy of jabs to the nose and eyes that completely disfigured Fontinato's face. But what hurt Fontinato that night was more than physical pain from a badly broken nose and cheekbone: His once-proud reputation of invincible indestructibility was severely tarnished.

They say that Fontinato was never the same after that incident, his confidence all but shattered. Players around the league no longer feared him and, shortly thereafter, the Rangers dealt him off to Montreal, where his career ended swiftly and suddenly, when he suffered a broken neck in a checking incident near the end boards against, ironically, his old team — the New York Rangers.

The Rocket's Double-Decker

There is no question that the great Maurice "Rocket" Richard rightfully earned his reputation as one of hockey's all-time greatest scorers. As a prolific pointmaker, he was subjected to the normal abuse from the league's tough guys: tripping, holding, wrestling, tugging, etc. But Richard was well equipped for any physical challenges he might encounter. Unbeknownst to many, he had once boxed in Golden Gloves competitions as a teen. The experience he gained from his early fighting days would come in handy one night when Les Canadiens visited New York for a game with the Rangers.

New York heavy Bob "Killer" Dill was assigned to shadow Rocket, and it wasn't long before tempers flared and fists were clenched. Dill was a renowned brawler whose penchant for intimidation was legitimate. But in their first encounter of the evening, Richard went after Dill in a free-for-all involving others, and KO'd him with a right to the jaw. When Dill revived, both were sent off the ice for fighting.

But it didn't end there.

Once in the penalty box (there were no separating partitions back then), the indignant Dill began to provoke Richard some more. Like déjà vu all over again, Rocket powdered Dill with yet another knockout punch and the Ranger defenseman fell from sight behind the penalty bench. Two KOs for Richard in one period of play!

The Rocket Richard Riot

It is considered one of the most extraordinary and violent events in hockey history and, again, involved the fiery high-scoring Maurice Richard of the Montreal Canadiens.

On March 13, 1955, with playoff tension hanging in the air at Boston Garden, the Canadiens were down 4–2 in their match against the Bruins, with just six minutes remaining. Montreal pulled its goalie early to add another forward to its front line with Boston already a man short due to a penalty. With a two-man advantage then, Richard brought the puck up ice. Just across the Boston blueline, he was slashed in the face from the stick of the Bruins' Hal Laycoe. Richard went ballistic. Swinging his stick over his head like a woodchopper, the enraged Canadien began pummeling Laycoe. Linesmen attempted to intervene between the two, one of them grabbing Richard's stick, but the Rocket could not be contained. Grabbing a loose stick on the ice, Richard renewed the attack once more. Again the linesman, Cliff Thompson, wrestled Richard away from Laycoe, ultimately pinning him to the ice. When Richard finally got loose, with the aid of a Canadiens teammate, he took a swing at Thompson, flooring the linesman!

The berserk Rocket was tossed from the game and, three days later, suspended for the balance of the season by league president Clarence Campbell, including the playoffs.

The evening following the unpopular announcement, on St. Patrick's Day in Montreal, Campbell unwisely chose to attend the Canadiens-Detroit Red Wings game at The Forum. Police had to use tear gas to keep the hostile crowd at bay from physically assaulting Campbell. Because The Forum had to be evacuated due to the gas, the Canadiens were required to forfeit the game. Upon hearing *that* news, the mob moved into full-scale riot mode, breaking windows and vandalizing stores outside the arena on St. Catherine Street. More than 50 stores were trashed, with damages estimated at over $100,000. Thirty-seven people were arrested.

Only an impassioned plea for order the following day from Richard, on both radio and television, restored the city to relative calm.

Karmic Law and the Green-Maki Incident

Boston Bruins defenseman Ted Green, nick-named "Terrible Ted" for his intimidating style of play, had reigned as one of hockey's leading badmen for eight years. He was so unpopular outside Boston that spectators used to throw flashlight batteries at him from the balconies. But on September 21, 1969, in a meaningless exhibition game, the tables were turned on Green as St. Louis Blues left winger Wayne Maki first slashed then speared the Boston defenseman, who retaliated both times. With the escalation of each exchange, Maki quantum-leaped to the next level, viciously pole-axing Green on top of the head with his stick. Green crumpled to the ice, his skull fractured. Surgeons required two delicate operations to remove skull fragments from Green's brain. His left side was paralyzed. Life itself hung in the balance.

After sitting out the 1969 season and missing the Bruins' first Stanley Cup title in 29 years, Green miraculously returned to the ice and contributed to the Bruins' Cup win in 1972.

In what some might view as a karmic-like "what goes around comes around," Maki died five years after the gruesome incident — ironically, from a brain tumor.

Janet Jones Gets Smashed

Almost everyone knows of Wayne Gretzky's marriage to actress Janet Jones, who gained fame for her role in *The Flamingo Kid,* among other screen credits. Although she starred in some hit movies, there is one hit she presumably would have wished had never happened.

On Wednesday night, October 22, 1997, while seated rinkside at Madison Square Garden in New York watching her husband play against the Chicago Blackhawks, the lights went out for Mrs. Gretzky. In a bizarre incident, Jones was knocked unconscious by a 6' x 6', 30-pound piece of Plexiglas that had become seriously disrupted from its moorings by a Blackhawks player, who was ridden by Rangers defenseman Ulf Samuelsson into the sideboards right in front of Jones' seat.

The quick trip to Dreamland for Jones resulted in a concussion and a split lip. Gretzky appeared disgusted with the incident, his scowling countenance making no attempt to hide his dissatisfaction with the Garden's malfunctioning armament.

This is not only a victory for the Canadiens; it is a victory for hockey. I hope that this era of intimidation and violence that is hurting our national sport is coming to an end. Young people have seen that a team can play electrifying, fascinating hockey while still behaving like gentlemen.

Serge Savard,
Montreal Canadiens defenseman (1966-81),
after his team had blanked the
bully-like Philadelphia Flyers
in the 1976 Stanley Cup Finals

Chapter 8

THE SIX ALL-TIME GREATEST TEAMS

I'll tell you how good Phil Esposito is. When you're playing against Espo, you start at least one goal down.

Punch Imlach,
Toronto Maple Leafs coach & general manager (1958-69);
general manager, Buffalo Sabres (1970-79)

He is the greatest goaltender I've ever seen.

Vladislav Tretiak,
legendary Soviet national team goalie,
on Gerry Cheevers

Not since the Rocket's heyday had any player dominated games the way Orr did, and no defenseman had ever so powered an offense, not even (Eddie) Shore.

Neil D. Isaacs,
author, Checking Back

6.

Boston Bruins (1969-78)

Just as hockey's Golden Age ended and the new-and-improved NHL took off with a six-team expansion in 1967-68, the perennial cellar-dwelling Boston Bruins staged one of pro hockey's enduringly great revivals. Basically, it was summed up in two words: Bobby Orr.

The arrival of the young 18-year-old phenom signaled a massive change in fortune for the long-suffering Bruins. Already in place were talented goaltender Gerry Cheevers and veteran Johnny Bucyk. All that was missing was scoring punch in the middle. Highly promising Blackhawks center Phil Esposito became available after an uninspiring playoff performance for Chicago and the Bruins got their much-needed scorer. In the 1969-70 season, Boston soared to the apex of hockey as Stanley Cup champions.

Much has been written of Orr, one of the game's true pioneering geniuses. It was his revolutionary approach to defense, his stunning presence as a rushing defenseman, that changed the way hockey is played forever. The game has never seen his equal, before or since.

The following year, Esposito obliterated the NHL single-season scoring record, but Boston failed to win the Stanley Cup. A year later though, in 1971-72, they were back on top, taking their second Cup in three years.

Boston should have remained a power long into the '70s, but the arrival of a new league, the World Hockey Association, and the continuing deterioration of Orr's sorry knees had a larger say. After Esposito was shipped off to the Rangers in '75, it was all but over. The golden ore of the Golden Orr Era had been thoroughly mined.

The Cup wasn't won in New York City. It belongs on Long Island.

Billy Smith,
New York Islanders goalie,
when a reporter mentioned that the Islanders
were the first New York team in 40 years
to win a Stanley Cup,
1980

I knew I had to be patient. It was like raising children. Bill Torrey's philosophy was to go with the youngsters, and I agreed that was where our future would be.

Roy Boe,
owner, New York Islanders,
1975

5.

New York Islanders (1979-84)

A common practice employed by established NHL teams, during the league's first wave of expansion in the late 1960s and early '70s, was to lure the new clubs into trading their top draft picks in exchange for worn-out war-torn veterans. It created the illusion of giving the yearling clubs instant stability, but in reality the future was sacrificed for the immediate present.

One of the teams who resisted that singing siren was the New York Islanders. With general manager Bill Torrey in firm control, the Islanders slowly built a powerhouse. Torrey started first with defense, acquiring goalie Billy Smith, the first NHL goalie from the 1980s to be inducted into the Hall of Fame, in the league's expansion draft. Smith would be the only original Islander still around when the club's run of four straight Stanley Cups began in 1979-80.

Next came stellar five-time first-team All-Star defenseman Denis Potvin, the first overall pick of the 1973 draft. Center Bryan Trottier was added in '75. He would exceed 100 points a season for five consecutive years. High-scoring right winger Mike Bossy, chosen late in 1977, would register a phenomenal 50 goals per season for nine straight seasons.

Smith was the on-ice leader. His patented hacking at opponents near the goal inspired a toughness in the Islanders that finally pushed them to the top in 1979-80. For four years in a row they reigned as Stanley Cup champs, before a young team from Edmonton, led by a guy named Gretzky, dethroned them.

He's a Rembrandt on the ice, a Nijinsky at the goalmouth.

Vincent D. Lunny,
Montreal author,
on Syl Apps

He could tend goal in a tornado and never blink an eye.

Jack Adams,
Detroit Red Wings coach (1927-47)
and general manager (1927-63),
on Maple Leafs goalie Turk Broda

Kennedy seldom lost an important face-off and was never beaten.

Fred Shero,
New York Rangers defenseman (1947-50)
and former Philadelphia Flyers
and New York Rangers coach

4.

Toronto Maple Leafs (1941-1951)

In the late 1940s, the Toronto Maple Leafs became the first team in National Hockey League history to win three consecutive Stanley Cups (1947-49). Over a ten-year span, from 1942 to 1951, the dominant Leafs took six Cups and were clearly considered the dynasty of the '40s.

With stars like center Syl Apps, wings Nick Metz and Sweeney Schriner, and goalie Turk Broda, the Leafs began their run at the top. It started with the 1941-42 season that climaxed with the greatest comeback in Stanley Cup history (see page 92). After defeating Detroit again three years later in 1945 for its second Cup of the decade, Toronto went about carving its record place in NHL history.

By this time, Ted Kennedy was on the scene, Apps' future replacement at center, as well as the team's future captain. Exciting new blood was also added in headhunter Bill Ezinicki and loose-cannon defenseman Hollywood Bill Barilko (see page 144). Again, the solid Broda was in goal. A characteristic of these Leafs was their capacity to become over-achievers come playoff time.

They could well have been called the "No-name Maple Leafs": Unaccountably, during their spotless three-year period in the late 1940s, only one Leafs player — Turk Broda — was selected as a first-team All-Star (1948).

Kurri is by far our most complete player. If he doesn't win the Selke Trophy (best defensive forward), they should throw it in the garbage.

Barry Fraser,
Edmonton Oilers scout,
March 1983

He had the sparkle in his eyes where others have glass.

Oilers coach Glen Sather,
on Wayne Gretzky

I call him a 747. When he's flying on the ice, he moves the air. He makes the rink look small.

Jean Perron,
Montreal Canadiens coach (1985-88),
on Mark Messier

The last great dynasty was the Ming dynasty. Not us.
Glen Sather

3.

Edmonton Oilers (1982-90)

They may have had the greatest player in the world but the Edmonton Oilers flaunted a support staff that rivaled any in NHL history.

In 1979, the year that four straggling World Hockey Association teams joined the established league, the Oilers struck gold in the amateur entry draft, nabbing defenseman Kevin Lowe, ebullient left winger/center Mark Messier, and right winger Glenn Anderson. A year later, Edmonton pulled in rushing defenseman Paul Coffey and brilliant Finnish skater Jarri Kurri. The year after that, they picked goalie Grant Fuhr. By the opening of the 1981-82 season, the Oilers' core group was in place.

And of course, the nucleus of the Edmonton universe, the great Wayne Gretzky, vibrated at the center of it all, winning an unimaginable eight successive league MVP awards upon his entrance into the National Hockey League.

In just their fourth season in the NHL, the Oilers made the Stanley Cup Finals. In true dynasty fashion, over the next seven seasons they would claim five Stanley Cups — the last one *without* Gretzky.

Too soon the old gang broke up. By the conclusion of the 1993-94 season, when the New York Rangers won their first Stanley Cup in 54 years, seven former Stanley Cup-winning Oilers from the great '80s teams dotted the New York roster, the most visible being captain Mark Messier.

There's one helluva lot more to being a tough guy than getting in a few phony fights where no real punches are tossed. To me being tough includes going into the corners without phoning ahead to see who's there.

Ted Lindsay,
Detroit Red Wings eight-time first-team NHL All-Star

It was said of Terry Sawchuk that he wasn't a whole man, rather, he was stitched together — held in place by catgut and surgical tape.

Stan and Shirley Fischler,
authors, Fischler's Ice Hockey Encyclopedia

If I had played with Gordie Howe my whole life I'd have 3000 points by now.

Wayne Gretzky,
1990

2.

Detroit Red Wings (1948-55)

It was an assemblage of some of the greatest talent the game has ever known. But the Detroit Red Wings' dynasty of the early 1950s — winners of four Stanley Cups in six years — quickly and sadly decomposed under the misguided trades of an impetuous owner whose nickname said it all: "Trader Jack" Adams.

Led by the famed "Production Line" of veteran center Sid Abel, Gordie Howe on the right, and left winger "Terrible" Ted Lindsay, Detroit set a league record of seven consecutive regular-season titles from 1948-55, an NHL mark that still stands. In five of those years the league scoring leader was a member from the "Line."

Defensively, the Red Wings were quarterbacked by Red Kelly, the first-ever Norris Trophy winner. In goal was the gifted Terry Sawchuk, a three-time Vezina Trophy winner during his days in Detroit. Five out of the starting six players on that team today are in the Hockey Hall of Fame. Howe, Lindsay, Kelly and Sawchuk were first-team All-Stars at least three times each during that run.

But in the 1955 off-season, after the Red Wings' third Stanley Cup championship in four years, Adams dealt Sawchuk to Boston in a stunning move. Two years later, for the unpardonable sin of attempting to start a league players' association, Lindsay was traded, along with up-and-coming goaltending superstar Glenn Hall, to Chicago. Sawchuk would later return for seven more productive years. Unfortunately, the same could not be said of the Red Wings as a team — their radiant time in the sun all too quickly expired.

The playing of Béliveau is poetry in action.

Hugh MacLennan,
Canadian novelist

The Rocket (was) the epitome of recklessness, of untrammeled fire and fury and abandon on the ice.

Peter Gzowski,
writer,
on Maurice Richard

He's a chippy operator...not unmindful of (Boston's) Milt Schmidt.

Jim Vipond,
Toronto Globe and Mail,
on Dickie Moore

1.

Montreal Canadiens — 1955-60

Whenever talk surfaces of the great Canadiens dynasty, the logical question arises, *Which one?*

The Habs have fielded hockey's most consistently brilliant teams. As 24-time winners of the Stanley Cup, the Canadiens are the unchallenged kings of the sport. No less than four dynasties dot the pages of Montreal's illustrious history.

Between 1916 and 1932, early-era stars Newsy Lalonde, Aurèle Joliat, Howie Morenz and goalies Georges Vezina and George Hainsworth led the Canadiens to four Stanley Cups. In the mid- to late 1960s, Montreal took four Cups behind the play of Jean Béliveau, Henri "Pocket Rocket" Richard, Yvan Cournoyer, and the rejuvenated Gumper, Lorne Worsley, in the nets. Six Stanley Cups were hoisted during the '70s, powered by Steve Shutt, Jacques Lemaire, and six-time first-team All-Star Guy Lafleur, the Canadiens' all-time leading scorer; with sensational Ken Dryden tending goal.

But there was nothing ever quite like those Canadiens of the '50s. Their starting lineup read like an all-time Who's Who: Maurice "Rocket" Richard, Dickie Moore, and Bernie "Boom Boom" Geoffrion at the wings; Béliveau at center; Doug Harvey and Tom Johnson on defense; and the great Jacques Plante in goal. That team to this day still holds the all-time Stanley Cup record for consecutive crowns — five in a row— from 1956-1960.

Once you wear the Canadiens sweater, you don't ever want to take it off again.

Pierre Larouche,
Montreal Canadiens (1977-82)

Chapter 9

OVERTIME

The Rocket's Red Glare

Maurice Richard was the most exciting athlete I have ever seen. So much has been written about Richard that for me to offer a flood of new praise would be roughly equivalent to a Ph.D. candidate announcing he is going to prove *Hamlet* is an interesting play.

Anonymous Canadian writer

I am me, not my brother. Maurice is the best hockey player of all time.

Henri Richard,
Montreal Canadiens (1955-1975)

Before Gordie Howe established himself, Richard was considered the Babe Ruth of hockey, and even after Gordie became the NHL's top scorer there were lots of debates about who was the better player, Howe or Richard. Gordie was a better all-around player and a better checking forward, but the one thing Richard had in more abundance than Howe was fire. The Rocket had dynamite in him.

Red Kelly,
Detroit Red Wings six-time All-Star defenseman

"He Shoots...He Scores!"

The time-honored hockey phrase "He shoots...he scores!" originated way back on March 22, 1923. Foster Hewitt, then a young reporter, rendered the historic words in what most people have come to believe was the first radio broadcast of a hockey game.

However, a 1972 story by *Regina Leader-Post* reporter Ron Campbell states that a radio broadcast on station CKCK of a Western Canada Hockey League playoff game between Edmonton and Regina, called by Pete Parker, took place on March 14, 1923 — nine days before Hewitt's well-recorded call of a senior game between Parkdale and Kitchener from Toronto's Mutual St. Arena.

Whichever claim is correct, it doesn't diminish Hewitt's contribution: His intense, infectious, climactic phrase gloriously hailing the bending of the hemp still rings to this day.

I caught lightning in a beer bottle.

Bill Mosienko,
Chicago Blackhawks, March 23, 1952,
after he scored three goals in 21 seconds
against the New York Rangers

A Masked Snake Named Jake

On November 1, 1959, Montreal Canadiens goalie Jacques Plante caught a flying puck with his face one time too many. This occasion, a blistering slap shot off the stick of the New York Rangers' Andy Bathgate from just 15 feet out, changed the game of hockey forever. After heading to the locker room for seven stitches to close the wound, Plante returned — wearing a mask. It didn't catch on right away, but in time, every goalie in the world would wear one.

Interestingly, Plante was not the originator of the mask in the NHL. Ottawa's Clint Benedict wore one in 1930 after a Howie Morenz shot had broken his nose. And in 1947, Rangers Hall of Fame goalie Chuck Rayner wore a plexiglass-type protective mask to let a fractured cheekbone heal. Both goalies tossed their masks afterwards, fearing, as Plante experienced, ridicule. The macho sport of hockey is merciless on the player not perceived as a warrior.

Plante's evolutionary path to the mask began after close encounters with pucks in 1954 and '55 fractured both cheekbones and his nose. A welder's mask sent by a fan proved way too cumbersome. Then, in 1958, Fiberglas Canada, Ltd. contacted Plante about a light, unbreakable, close-fitting prototype mask the company had developed. Though ready for the 1959-60 season, the mask's use was initially discouraged by Canadiens' coach Toe Blake, who feared Plante's vision would be limited. But then Nov. 1st dawned and hockey's new day began.

Plante went on to win the Vezina Trophy that year.

The Amazing Barilko Coincidence

A hockey hero and his team's success in Stanley Cup play are entwined for eternity.

In August 1951, little did Toronto defenseman Hollywood Bill Barilko know that he was about to become an instant legend, give or take 11 years.

Barilko earlier that spring had starred in the Leafs' Stanley Cup Finals victory over Montreal, scoring the decisive game- and series-winning goal in overtime. He had been on a fishing trip and was returning to his home in Timmons, when a float-plane that was transporting him and a friend disappeared north of Cochrane, Ontario. Barilko's and the plane's whereabouts remained a mystery.

Eleven years passed after Barilko's Stanley Cup heroics and his subsequent disappearance before Toronto won another Stanley Cup, at the conclusion of the 1962 season.

Oddly, not long after that victory, the crash site and Barilko's body were found.

The Great One

Hey, you're not the greatest! *I* am the greatest!

> *Muhammad Ali,*
> *to Wayne Gretzky*

I'd always wanted to wear *9*, because Gordie Howe wore it. One day (my coach) told me, "Why don't you wear *99?*"

> *Wayne Gretzky,*
> *on choosing a jersey number*
> *with his first professional club,*
> *Sault Ste. Marie*

The players I most admired in my life are Bobby Orr, Gordie Howe, and Jean Béliveau.

> *Wayne Gretzky*

He could snap a puck through a refrigerator door.

> *Wayne Gretzky,*
> *on Mario Lemieux*

Hockey's First Black Player

Willie O'Ree, a right winger for the Boston Bruins, became the Jackie Robinson of hockey in 1957-58 — the first black man to play in the NHL. Though not quite performing to the level of Robinson's phenomenal abilities, O'Ree scored four goals and 10 assists for the Bruins in his second stint with the team, during the 1960-61 season. He played a total of 45 games in his two years with Boston, playing out the remainder of his hockey career in the minors.

The Great Zamboni

In the late 1940s, a Californian named Frank Zamboni experimented with cleaning and resurfacing the ice at a skating rink that he was operating by having a tractor pull a sled across the ice.

In 1949, the well-known intermission "entertainment" for hockey fans made its debut. Using a 2.3-litre engine powered by propane, the Zamboni scrapes off a thin layer of ice, heats the surface, then drops freshly heated water that freezes within ten minutes to form a new layer of ice. The life expectancy of a Zamboni is relatively short, a little less than your own car's career — about five years. Each "flood" requires about 275 litres of hot water. On the average, The Bone administers about 2,000 floodings a year.

Maple Leaf Gardens first used a Zamboni in 1962. Prior to that, the ice was cleared by hand and barrels full of hot water were pushed around the rink. The Toronto facility thus became the first NHL arena to provide fresh floods between periods.

Conspicuous Consumption

During an average season, a Toronto Maple Leafs player will go through 240 hockey sticks, will have his skates sharpened 125 times, and will wear through five pairs of padded gloves. Over the course of a season, the Leafs will guzzle almost 2,000 litres of Gatorade, wrap themselves in 7,500 rolls of tape, wear down 2,000 bars of soap and chew 30,000 sticks of gum.

What Do All-Stars Doug Harvey and Denis Potvin Have in Common?

Both Doug Harvey and Denis Potvin, brilliant all-time all-star defensemen, have had the dubious distinction of inadvertently scoring goals *against* their own teams in critical playoff action.

They've assassinated soccer players in Colombia for such actions.

In the first game of the 1979-80 Stanley Cup Finals, against Patrick Division-rival Philadelphia, the New York Islanders' Potvin accidentally pushed the puck into his own net, in an attempt to stuff it for safekeeping under goalie Billy Smith. However, fate was kind to Potvin: an opportunity arose at 4:07 of overtime for the New York defenseman to score the winning goal, giving the Islanders a critical 4–3 Game 1 win at Philadelphia. It set the tone for the remainder of the series, as the Islanders went on to take the first of their four straight Stanley Cups.

Harvey wasn't so fortunate. In overtime of Game 7 of the 1953-54 Stanley Cup Finals, Detroit's Tony Leswick lifted a soft dump shot toward the Montreal goal. Harvey attempted to glove the puck, but it bounced off his thumb and over the shoulder of Canadiens goalie Gerry McNeil. Game over. Cup to Detroit.

On the Noble Art of Goaltending

My business is getting shot at.

Jacques Plante,
Montreal Canadiens,
four other teams (1952-65; 1968-73)

Only Dunlop has seen more rubber than I have.

Dominik Hasek,
Chicago Blackhawks (1990-92),
Buffalo Sabres (1992-)

To the approaching offensive player, the goalie wearing his portable fort and breastplate of raw guts looks like a man-eating giant. He eats raw hockey pucks, salted or not.

Chandler W. Sterling,
author

I stitch better when my skin is smooth.

Lorne Chabot,
New York Rangers (1926-28),
Toronto Maple Leafs (1928-33),
Montreal Canadiens (1933-34),
Chicago Blackhawks (1934-35),
on why he shaves before games

Today everybody has a slap shot, and they're the most dangerous. The curve can drive a goalie crazy — or kill him. It makes the puck rise, drop, sail off — a knuckle ball at 100 mph. If a man ever gets control of the curved stick, the goalies would be better off blowing their brains out before they get knocked out. This way it's a slow death at best.

Tony Esposito,
Chicago Blackhawks (1969-84)

Sixty minutes of hell.

Glenn Hall,
Detroit Red Wings (1952-53; 1954-57),
Chicago Blackhawks (1957-67),
St. Louis Blues (1967-71)

How would you like it if you were sitting in your office and you made one little mistake? Suddenly, a big red light goes on behind you and 18,000 people jump up and start screaming at you...calling you a bum and an imbecile. Then they start throwing a lot of garbage at you. Well, that's what it's like when you play goal for an NHL team.

Jacques Plante

Playing goal is a winter of torture for me.

Glenn Hall,
who played 502 games in goal,
from 1955-62, without missing a game

There is no position in sports as noble as that of goaltending.

Vladislav Tretiak,
legendary Central Red Army Team (USSR) goalie (1969-84)

Wayne, get me job as American fullback.

Vladislav Tretiak,
to Wayne Gretzky,
on Tretiak's secret desire to become an NFL fullback

The only job worse is a javelin catcher at a track-and-field meet.

Lorne "Gump" Worsley,
New York Rangers (1952-53; 1954-63),
Montreal Canadiens (1963-70),
Minnesota North Stars (1970-74)

All of us in Washington can appreciate what goalies do — we have so many shots taken at us.

Bill Clinton,
42nd president of the United States

BIBLIOGRAPHY

&

INDEX

Bibliography

Berger Gilda. Violence and Sports. New York: Franklin Watts, 1990.

Davidson, John and John Steinbreder. Hockey For Dummies. Foster City, CA: IDG Books Worldwide, Inc., 1997.

Davis, Karen and Michael Kuta, ed. Hockeytown — Detroit Red Wings 1997-98 Media Guide. North American Graphics, 1997.

Dryden, Ken. Face-Off at the Summit. USA: Sports Illustrated, 1973.

Fischler, Stan and Shirley Walton. The Hockey Encyclopedia — The Complete Record of Professional Ice Hockey. New York: Macmillan Publishing Co., 1983.

Fischler, Stan and Shirley, Morgan Hughes, Joseph Romain, James Duplacey. 20th Century Hockey Chronicle. Lincolnwood, Illinois: Publications International, Ltd., 1994.

Fischler, Stan. Motor City Muscle. Toronto: Warwick Publishing, Inc., 1996.

Fischler, Stan and Shirley. Fischler's Revised Edition Ice Hockey Encyclopedia. New York: Thomas Y. Crowell Company, 1979.

Freeman, Brad, ed. The Blackhawks 97-98 Cold Steel on Ice Media Guide. USA: 1997.

Gretzky, Wayne. Gretzky, An Autobiography. New York: HarperCollins, 1990.

Hockey Hall of Fame Library. Grand Old Houses of Hockey. Toronto: 1998.

Holland, Heidi. Boston Bruins 1997-98 Guide and Record Book. MA: Treetop Graphics, 1997.

Hollander, Zander and Mike Emrick. Inside Sports Hockey. Detroit: Visible Ink Press, 1998.

Hunter, Douglas. Champions — The Illustrated History of Hockey's Greatest Dynasties. Chicago: Triumph, 1997.

Inglis, Greg, ed. The National Hockey League Guide &

Record Book 1997-98. Chicago: Triumph Books, 1997.

Isaacs, Neil D. Checking Back. New York: W.W. Norton & Company, Inc., 1977.

Knowles, Steve. 1997-98 Oilers Official Guide. Edmonton Oilers, 1997.

Liebman, Glenn. Hockey Shorts. Chicago: Contemporary Books, 1996.

McFarlane, Brian. Everything You've Always Wanted to Know About Hockey. New York: Charles Scribner's Sons, 1971.

McFarlane, Brian. The Stanley Cup. New York: Charles Scribner's Sons, 1971.

McFarlane, Brian. The Story of the National Hockey League. New York: Charles Scribner's Sons, 1973.

McFarlane, Brian. The Best of It Happened in Hockey. Toronto: Stoddart Publishing Co. Limited, 1997.

NHL Communications Group. The NHL Official Guide & Record Book 1992-93. Toronto: NHL, 1992.

Park, Patrick, ed. 1997-98 Official Guide to Toronto Maple Leafs. Spalding Creative Communications, 1997.

Rosasco, John, ed. Rangers 1997-98 Media Guide. Command Color Press, 1997.

Saillant, Dominick, ed. Canadiens 1997-98. Canada: Québécor, Inc., 1997.

Sterling, Chandler W. The Icehouse Gang. New York: Charles Scribner's Sons, 1972.

Sullivan, George. Face-Off! Princeton, Toronto, Melbourne, London: D. Van Nostrand Company, Inc., 1968.

Trammel, Jeff and Tony Ommen. St. Louis Blues Official Yearbook 1997-98. St. Louis, MO., 1997.

Index

Index

About the Author

Alan Ross is a sports historian and writer living in Monteagle, Tennessee. A graduate of Fordham University, he is a former editor for Professional Team Publications, Athlon Sports Communications, and Walnut Grove Press. His feature articles on sports history have appeared in *The Sporting News*, *Lindy's*, *Athlon Sports*, *Athletic Administration*, *Game Day*, *NFL Insider*, *Arizona Cardinals Media Guide, and Track Record*. In addition, he is the history columnist for *Oilers Exclusive*, the official publication of the Tennessee Oilers. He has authored four other books, *A Brief History of Golf, Golf à la cart, Echoes from the Ball Park,* and *Love is Forever,* co-written with his wife, Karol.